Anja Jakob & Cordula Weiss

Games With Your Dog
For Indoors and Out

Mental exercise, tricks and games for every dog

Quiller

Picture sources:

Title photo: Maren Leuker
Photo of the author Cordula Weiss: private
Photo of the author Anja Jakob: Indian Eyes Photography by Daniela Juwan
All the other photos come from Silke Klewitz-Seemann.

The recommendations and information in this book have been compiled and checked extremely carefully by the authors. However, a guarantee cannot be given for the accuracy of the information. The authors and publisher do not assume any liability for losses and accidents. Please use your own personal judgement when applying the recommendations in this book.

The publisher is not responsible for the content of the websites mentioned in the book.

Copyright © Anja Jakob and Cordula Weiss 2024

© 2022 by Eugen Ulmer KG, Stuttgart, Germany
First published in Germany as *Hundespiele für Drinnen und Draussen*

English Language Edition © Quiller Publishing 2024

British Library Cataloguing-in-Publication Data
A catalogue record for this book is available from the British Library.

ISBN 978 1 84689 386 5 (paperback)
ISBN 978 1 84689 387 2 (e-book)

The right of Anja Jakob and Cordula Weiss to be identifed as the authors of this work has been asserted in accordance with the Copyright, Design and Patent Act 1988.

All rights reserved. No part of this book may be reproduced or transmitted in any form or by any means, electronic or mechanical including photocopying, recording or by any information storage and retrieval system, without permission from the Publisher in writing.

Production: Stephanie Haun
Cover design: siegel konzeption | gestaltung, Stuttgart
Set: r&p digitale medien, Echterdingen
Reproduction: time:ray, Jettingen
Translator: Gloria Brian

Printed in China

Quiller

An imprint of Amberley Publishing
The Hill, Merrywalks, Stroud, GL5 4EP
Tel: 01453 847800
E-mail: info@quillerbooks.com
Website: www.quillerpublishing.com

About the Authors

Anja Jakob has specialised in games, sport and fun for intelligent dogs with her Anja Jakob dog training school – "creative games lead to playful success" (www.anjajakob.com). In addition to trick training, retrieving, thinking and sniffing games, she also focuses on the German game of "Treibball" (where the dog has to gather and move large exercise balls into a football goal), creative lunging, impulse control games, dog dancing and pulling games for dogs. She also runs seminars at dog training schools and clubs as well as training weeks in dog hotels.

Cordula Weiss breeds short-haired collies and it's very important to her that her dogs are kept busy in a variety of ways. Her passion is to combine positive dog training with enjoyable exercise and thinking. As a dog breeder and website author (www.kalalassies.de), she can always be contacted for anything to do with dogs and feels she has an obligation to help people and dogs get on well together.

Anja Jakob

Games to Play Inside

Playing Inside?   10

Mental Exercise   12

    Treats' Maze   14
    Bottle Rolling   16
    Thimblerig   18
    Treat Mikado   20
    Bottle Turning   22
    Flying Saucers   24
    Surprising Tubes   26

Retrieving Games   28

    Mine or Yours?   30
    High Stacking   32
    I'm Packing   34
    Search & Bring   36

Rediscover Children's Games With Your Dog   38

    Ball Catcher   40
    Fishing for Ducks   42
    Letter Mash-up   44
    Stacking Rings   46
    Playing Football   48

All Kinds of Tricks 50

Hello!	52
High Five	54
High Ten	56
All Good Things Come in Threes	58
Let's Jump!	60
Feet	62
Hide	64
Skateboarding	66
Back up	68

Your Dog as Your Helper 70

A Visitor?	72
Oh, it's Dark in Here	74
Take it	76
On Your Socks	78
Socks Off!	80
Messenger Service	82

Cordula Weiss

Games to Play Outside

Let's go Outside!	86
Practical Information	88

Ignore Joggers	90
Stay Cool	92
A Nice Back…	94
Achoo!	96
Good Idea	98
Sniffing Around	100
Playing Sherpa	102

Games Involving Exercise — 104

Twist and Turn	106
Obstacle Course	108
Triathlon	110
Round, Round, Get Around	112
Well Herded!	114
Slalom	116

Impulse Control — 118

Catch it!	120
Balla-balla!	122
One, Two, Three, Hide!	124
Come Here!	126
Chase the Prey	128

Works of Art   **130**

Target!	132
The Trick Bench	134
The Naysayer	136
Catch the Dog	138
Cool Paw	140
My Dog, the Model	142
Into the Blue	144

Nose Work   **146**

Finders, Keepers	148
Let's Search!	150
Where is he?	152
Picnic on the Grass	154
Show me!	156
Geocaching	158

Resources   **160**

Further Reading and Websites   160

Games to Play Inside

Playing Inside?

You and your dog are bound to enjoy being outside with nature, going for long walks and keeping busy outdoors. However, there are always days when it would be nice for a short stroll to be sufficient without feeling guilty. For example, when you have workmen in the home, are spring cleaning, have to work in your office for several hours, wait for another delivery or your dog is ill and can't walk far, the weather outside is pretty awful or…

In this book you will find lots of ideas and suggestions so that your dog can quickly let off steam in your own four walls and then have a nap in his basket to give you more time for other things. Of course, your dog won't mind if you simply also play with him at home just for fun now and then – even though you spend a lot of time together being out and about every day…

Clicking, Marker Signal or Word of Praise & Reward

For me, training by using positive reinforcement with a clicking sound, marker signal (such as a click of the tongue or word of praise) and treats is the most effective way of teaching dogs to follow your train of thought, increase their understanding and teach them something new. The symbol 👍 in the text always tells you when you should give your dog feedback via a clicking sound, marker signal or word of praise to show that he has done something correctly at the very moment when the clicking noise, marker signal or word of praise is sounded and will immediately receive a reward. This can be something to eat, but also a toy or other reward. The advantage is that you will gain at bit of time and don't have to have food in your hand when you are training your dog as it usually distracts dogs and prevents them from learning. After the immediate feedback, you still have enough time to put your hand in your pocket to give your dog the treat you have promised.

Without any food in front of them, dogs who are completely obsessed with food can concentrate better on the relevant exercises and learning stages. We humans are also not always rewarded immediately. Or does your boss continually wave banknotes in your face to motivate you to work? Although you would think this was great, it would prove to be a huge distraction. You also have to trust that the wages for your work will be paid – only your dog has the advantage that he doesn't have to wait until the end of the month…

Tips for Sceptics

The reward doesn't always have to be a treat but can sometimes also be a toy or something else which represents a reward for your dog at that very moment. In addition to a word of praise and treats, you can reward your dog by throwing a bag of food or toy for a change. Perhaps he also likes to be tickled behind his ears, on his tummy or played with? For some of the exercises in this book, your dog will also be busy with items such as rubber animals or socks – which is even a reward in itself for some dogs. At that very moment, he often won't even want a treat any more. However, if your dog thinks the items are actually too wonderful, and doesn't want to give them back, then swap this with his favourite toy or a very high value treat. Even if you would like to practise something new, challenging or have a little couch potato, who finds it very difficult to raise any enthusiasm for new exercises, you should also sometimes reward him with cubes of cheese or sausage or other treats which he only receives very rarely, in addition to the usual ones.

▼ I'm sooooo bored ...
Can't we do something?

At a glance

How easy is it to put the idea into practice? How time-consuming is it? How much space is needed? You will find this information next to every instruction.

Time needed:

 little

 medium

 lots

Level of difficulty:

 easy

 medium

 challenging

Space needed:

 little

 medium

 lots

The Pathway is the Aim

The more varied and surprising the training and the relevant rewards are, the more fun your dog will have and learn more enjoyably and quickly. However, the exercises are not about your dog learning them as quickly as possible, but rather that you both have as much fun together for as long as possible.

Mental Exercise

Something Quick for in Between

Dogs love games involving mental exercise. They really enjoy continually mastering new challenges to receive a reward. You are encouraged to join in and find creative new ways of solving the puzzles, which have been set. Specialist shops now offer a large selection of such puzzles – but unfortunately, they are usually quite expensive. I would, therefore, like to encourage you to merely be inspired by them and go through your attic, shed, garage or DIY store.

It's often quick and cheap to make games with similar items yourself and continually redesign them. Most of the tasks are similar. For example, the dogs have to push something to the side, lift it, press it down or pull it to be successful.

Treats' Maze *Search games & tongue gymnastics*

For whom? *1 person + 1 dog*
What resources? *Plant tray, various items*
Requirements? *None*

The Task:

Head off to your nearest garden centre for some of the plastic plant trays in which the flower pots are usually transported. You will normally be given them free of charge. There are lots of different versions, which continually set new challenges.

It's your dog's task to look for treats in the slots and fish them out with his tongue. This is sometimes not so easy because some plant trays have connecting channels so that the water is distributed better when the plants are watered. As a result, the treats are quite likely to move to the next section when attempts are made to remove them.

The smaller the diameter of the slots, the more difficult it is to get the treats out. On the other hand, it's relatively easy to push items underneath, which are placed on top as an additional obstacle. The larger the diameter of the slot, the deeper the items are and therefore the more difficult it is to remove them.

Step by Step:

1. Let your dog watch from a short distance while you fill the tray with treats. If necessary, tie him up or ask someone to hold him briefly.

2. If your dog doesn't like the look of the tray or if it's one of the first mental exercises for your dog, then place the treats on the edge to start with, but also put a few in the slots.

3. Place the tray in front of your dog, hold it firmly with one hand and ask him to search.

4. Encourage him repeatedly and praise him with your voice when he is successful and manages to fish out a treat.

5. The next step is for you to hide the treats under balls, toys or yoghurt pots, which you place on top of them. When you do this, you don't need to put a treat under every item. The point is for your dog to use his nose to search and have to make an effort.

6. Increase the level of difficulty from time to time. You can use heavy metal balls like those used to play boules or items which sit deeper in the holes – for example muffin baking tins made of silicone. Cut round slices out of a sponge or block of foam, which completely disappear into the openings or screw up newspaper, in which you also wrap up the treats.

7. Another option: hide various treats and find out which ones your dog likes the most.

▶ **A popular traditional game** for dogs with little experience of mental exercises, dogs lacking in confidence and puppies. The level of difficulty is variable, dogs also lose their shyness of unfamiliar items and noises and quickly become successful.

▶ Ridgeback-Dame Lucy using her nose.

Bottle Rolling *Affordable alternative to a feeding ball*

The Task:

Here your dog must find a way of reaching the treats in the bottles.

For whom? *1 person + 1 dog*

What resources? *Empty plastic bottles, nail scissors, sharp knife or cordless drill*

Requirements? *None*

Different version: Put treats in several bottles in the bottle carrier

As soon as your dog has worked out the task and the bottle is rolling around your home, you can make the exercise more difficult. Find some more bottles and put them in a bottle carrier. Now hide the treats both in and under the bottles. This will keep your dog occupied for much longer.

Step by Step:

1. Drill several holes into one of the empty plastic bottles. It's easiest to do this with a cordless drill. First use a thinner and then a thicker drill bit so that the plastic doesn't split. Alternatively, you can also use a sharp knife or nail scissors.

2. The diameter of the holes should be only slightly larger than the diameter of the treats you are using.

3. Smooth the sharp edges either with a sharp knife or by holding a flame from a lighter by the holes. Do this outside and hold the bottle up and the flame from below vertically in the relevant hole so that it remains round and not too much plastic melts.

4. Now you can put a few treats into the bottle and screw the top back on – your dog will certainly already be quite excited.

5. Then place or lay the bottle in front of your dog and wait to see what he does.

6. If he tries to bite the bottle, take it away again and say sadly "Shame!" After a few seconds give it back again.

7. If he wants to bite into the bottle again, hold the bottle tightly and show it to your dog. Praise him for as long as he carefully sniffs the bottle or paws at it.

8. Then place it on the floor again. He will soon understand that he is only supposed to nudge the bottle so that the treats fall out.

▶ **Australian Shepherd** puppy Trudy **investigating the new toy.**

Thimblerig *Slightly differently*

The Task:

Your dog should lift up cones, drinking beakers or yoghurt pots to receive a reward.

For whom? *1 person + 1 dog*

What resources? *For example, plastic beakers and bowls, small cones, etc.*

Requirements? *None*

Step by Step:

1. First play the traditional thimblerig game by hiding a treat under one of three upside-down beakers. Move them around secretly in front of your excited spectator before he is allowed to start searching.

2. Now it becomes more difficult – take one beaker in your hand and drop a treat into it. Hold the container in front of your dog so that he can try to fish it out with his tongue. Your dog is bound to have a very long tongue, so let him try for a while. If he really can't manage this because his nose is simply too wide, then look for a more suitable container.

3. The next stage is for your dog to have further to reach for his treat. Place a second beaker containing another treat on top of the first. This task is very likely to be solved very quickly.

4. Now place another treat in the beaker and put a second beaker inside it so that only a narrow edge is visible over the top. Your dog must now find a way of removing the upper beaker. Some dogs will push it away with their nose, gently take it out using their teeth or fish it out with their paws. In any case, hold the lower beaker firmly in your hands.

5. Think about additional challenges – for example two colanders, keys or two cones on top of each other.

▲ Hey presto – it is gone!

▼ Sandy – an enthusiastic thimblerig player.

Treat Mikado *Look in the tubes*

The Task:

In which tube are the treats hidden and how will your dog reach them?

For whom? *1 person + 1 dog*

What resources? *Cable ducts from a DIY store, drainpipe sections or yoghurt pots*

Requirements? *None*

Options for experts

Place several beakers with treats in a box. Short drainpipe sections from a DIY store, which you close at one end with a suitable stopper, are particularly good. They are more stable, don't split and have a narrower opening than yoghurt pots so that your dog has to remove them from the box and roll them to make the treats fall out.

Step by Step:

1. You can find cable ducts with various diameters in a DIY store – depending on how thick the treats are.

2. Saw the cable ducts into short and longer pieces. Alternatively, you can also use drainpipe sections, which are already available in various lengths and shapes.

3. Start with a very short piece, into which you place the treat – it must be able to be removed easily so that your dog has no reason to bite on the duct/tube. If he still tries to do this, take it away briefly and say "Shame".

4. Give it back to him again and as long as he only touches it with his nose or paws, rolls it or gently lifts it up with his teeth, praise him verbally.

5. If the short ducts/tubes are successful, gradually add increasingly longer pieces like Mikado.

6. The longer the ducts/tubes are, the more fiddly it becomes. If you place a folded blanket under the ducts/tubes, they and the treats won't roll away so easily and the treats will still fall out silently.

7. You can make it even more difficult by stuffing one end of the duct/tube with a piece of paper towel. This means that the treats will only fall out from one end or your dog will first have to pull out the paper.

8. You can also hide various kinds of treats in the ducts/tubes and see which your gourmet prefers and tries first.

9. Children also really enjoy playing this game.

Phoebe is wondering "It must be here somewhere?"

Bottle Turning Not for bottles

The Task:

Turn the bottle with his snout or paws using the stick so that a treat falls out.

For whom? 1 person + 1 dog

What resources? Empty sturdy plastic bottle, sharp knife/cordless drill, wooden spoon or stick

Requirements? None

Step by Step:

1. Drill two holes in the top half of the plastic bottle (as described on page 16) and place the wooden spoon or stick through them.

2. The bottle should therefore be heavier lower down and the bottleneck should still be pointing upwards.

3. If your clever clogs has already successfully mastered several mental exercises, simply hold the bottle in front of him, pop a treat into it and wait to see how he attempts to solve the new task.

4. If he bites the bottleneck, say "Shame!" and briefly hold the bottle away from him.

5. Of course, you could also help your dog. But it's supposed to be a mental exercise. It's therefore not about him learning as quickly as possible. Let him try things out – this will make it more enjoyable for both of you!

6. Otherwise, you could reaffirm every action by your dog, which should in principle be successful, by praising him and tipping the bottle yourself so that the treat falls out. Initially already reward every slight touch with his nose or hold the bottle horizontally with one hand and the other on top of it and encourage him to "give you his paw" (see pages 26 and 52). Then quickly pull your hand away so that his nose touches the bottle.

7. From time to time, you should now expect your clever four-legged friend to make more of an effort by nudging or stroking the bottle a few times with his paw before you turn it over for him. Soon he will be able to do it on his own.

▲ German shepherd mix Pearl has the hang of it.

▶ Soon it'll come flying out …

What should you do if your dog is frightened of the bottle and the noise it makes?

First hold the bottle with one hand without the stick horizontally in front of your dog and place a treat in the neck of the bottle. Every time he dares to move closer to the bottle, let a treat drop out. Soon he will then also have the courage to carefully touch the bottle with his tongue, then fish out the treats or nudge the bottle with his nose.

Flying Saucers *and treats*

The Task:

Your dog must pull out several discs from a bottle so that the treat falls out from the bottom.

For whom? *1 person + 1 dog*

What resources? *Plastic bottle, saw, kitchen knife, place set, scissors, pen, paper*

Requirements? *None*

Step by Step:

1. Saw several slits into a sturdy plastic bottle up to the middle in each case and smooth the sharp edges with a kitchen knife.

2. Push a piece of paper into the slit and draw the semicircle of the bottle with the pen. Now cut out discs of this size with the help of this template from thin cardboard or plastic place sets.

3. Throw a treat into the bottle and first push only one of the discs into the bottle. Then turn it over and hold it in front of your dog's nose.

4. Let him try to work out what he has to do this time – perhaps he will find the solution to the problem all on his own. Again, interrupt behaviour which is too excitable with "Shame!"

5. You can help by giving him a signal such as "Take it", "Bring" or "Pull" (see page 36).

6. Another option would be to place one of the discs onto a stool so that it protrudes slightly over the end of the seat. Push it back into the bottle and hold both towards him and say "Bring" again.

7. In this way it will slowly dawn on him what you want from him – now try it again with a treat and a disc in the bottle. As soon as this works, add more discs.

8. Let him start at the top so that the treat drops down one level after every disc is pulled out to increase the excitement.

◀ Just wait – I'll get you!

▶ **Pull by pull** towards the target.

Surprising Tubes

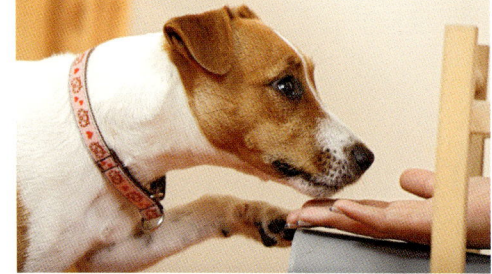

For whom? *1 person + 1 dog*

What resources? *Materials and implements in the construction instructions*

Requirements? *None*

The Task:

This game is slightly more elaborate to construct. Your four-legged friend's task is to press down the tubes in the structure and hold them still for a bit at the bottom until a treat or ball rolls out. He can press down the tubes with his nose or paws. However, it's not enough simply to nudge them or briefly paw at them. This is because the treat needs a bit of time until it has rolled to the exit. If your dog releases the tubes again full of expectation as soon as the treat starts to roll, the tube will accelerate upwards again and the treat will roll back to the lower end, where the tubes are closed. The sound this makes might also annoy him and he might go to the other side where he will, of course, look for the treat in vain.

Before you start this game, you will probably already have tried other mental exercises from this book with your dog, so you shouldn't really need to help him. He will find the solution to the puzzle and find out how the mechanism works at some point. And after you have created such a structure, your dog should enjoy playing with it for as long as possible, shouldn't he?

Step by Step:

You can find detailed illustrated instructions by using the link below to help you make the Surprising Tubes very easily: https://bitly.com/surprisingtubes. Of course, you can also be creative yourself and design your own version.

1. As soon as it is ready, your dog should watch how you make treats or a ball disappear into the tubes. Then it's his turn so just let him have a go.

2. He will really make an effort and enjoy trying because he knows from previous games that there is always a reward at the end. Your dog is bound to enjoy this more if he can find the solution on his own – without any help. It's the same for us humans.

3. After your clever dog has now discovered that he has only to hold the tubes down long enough until the treat has rolled out, you can make it more difficult. Think about new challenges. For example, hide a treat in one tube and then stuff it with rolled up kitchen paper, a sponge, a sock or a dummy on a string so that just a bit pokes

▶ Plop – "I can hear it, smell it … but how do I get to it?"

out of the tube. Your dog will again happily push the tubes down and wonder why nothing comes out this time. He must now find out why, and learn that the blockage must first be removed and only then when he presses down again will the deserved reward see the light of day.

4. Another version would be to encourage your dog and deliberately show a different form of behaviour than he would display of his own accord. If your dog wants to press the tubes down with his nose, practise so that he does this with his paw specifically in future in response to a corresponding signal.

5. Let your dog "sit" down in front of the tubes, hold your hand directly over the upper end of the tubes and encourage him to give you his paw (see page 52). As soon as his paw touches your hand, praise him and give him a treat from your other hand. The next time pull your hand back as soon as your dog goes towards it with his paw so that he touches the tubes with his paw instead. From now on give a reward only for this new behaviour – ignore the previous nudging with his nose.

6. If on the other hand, you have a little bruiser, who plays around with his paws on the tubes every time, teach him how to only press down with the tip of his nose in future in response to your signal "Nudge" (see page 48).

7. Most dogs are continually fascinated by the game, even if they have already understood the principle for a long time.

3, 2, 1 ... yours!
Retrieving Games

Retrieving games are some of the most popular ways of entertaining our dogs. Some dogs offer to do this of their own accord – others first have to learn it. However, usually we humans are not very imaginative and just say "Search and bring the ball". Lots of dogs really enjoy it if someone throws them something but they don't reliably bring it back every time.

In this chapter you will find out how you can teach your four-legged friend to reliably bring back toys to you and place them in your hands among other things. You can find other ideas where bringing items is the focus of the task in the chapter called "Rediscover Children's Games With Your Dog".

Mine or Yours? *Bring it to me please!*

For whom? *1 person + 1 dog*

What resources? *Objects to be retrieved*

Requirements? *None*

The Task:

Your dog should learn how to reliably place objects in your hand. A distinction must be made between dogs who have so far never retrieved anything and dogs who have seen objects thrown for them, but who don't come back with the object or don't want to return it. They cheerfully run after it, take the object, chew on it and want to play a tugging game with their owners or back off as soon you want to take the toy away from them.

If your dog has so far hardly taken anything into his mouth or is unhappy to do so, you need to find an object made from a material, which is as acceptable to your dog as possible. The size, material and also the shape play a role so try out various ones: rubber, fabric, fur fabric, wood, large, small, thick, thin or as light as possible. However, if you have the opposite problem that your dog will only fool around with the object for the sheer fun of it, then choose an item, which he finds much less exciting. In other words, instead of his favourite toy, find something made of metal such as a spoon.

Step by Step:

1. Hold the object you have selected in front of your dog and say "Take it". He might sniff at it immediately or chew it. You can also smear it with liver sausage.

2. Every time he touches the item: 👍 and from time to time expect more action from your dog until it is completely in his mouth. If your dog hasn't done any retrieving before, it may take several training sessions before he briefly takes the object in his mouth when you hold it in front of him.

Training tips:

- If your dog has a tendency to chew on the item or continually wants to play tugging games with you instead of quietly handing the object over to you, then first practise "Pattex".

- To do this, sit next to your dog and first place your open hand briefly under his chin = 👍. If you sit in front of him, he might confuse this with the paw-giving exercise. Every time try to leave your hand under his chin for a bit longer. It's easiest if you give him a treat while your hand is still resting under his chin – keep saying "Pattex". After a few repetitions, try to hold your hand three centimetres lower after having given the treat. Does he follow your hand down with his chin and try to make contact with your hand again? Bingo! Clever dog and of course 👍. The next step is to practise and say "Pattex", place your hand under his chin and put something to retrieve in his mouth. He can't

▶ Merlin is practising "Pattex" – and at the same time holding something calmly in his mouth.

simultaneously press his chin into your hand and chew or do other silly things with the object.

- Lots of dogs find it easier or simply enjoy it more if there are several objects to retrieve in the game and they don't have to place them directly in your hand. Try the following exercise. You need two rubber toy families in lots of different colours and shapes, which you will find in baby toy departments in stores.

- **Different versions:** arrange ducks and frogs according to colour – rubber toy families are great for retrieving. You can also use them to teach your dog how to distinguish various colours. At the beginning, depending on which of the small animals he approaches you with, hold the corresponding size towards him (see page 28). Later he will have to decide himself and arrange them correctly to receive a reward from you.

3. Hold the item firmly in your hand. Every time he briefly places his teeth around the item, say the word of praise and immediately "Out" and 👍. Praise him and give him a treat. If this is attractive enough, even a dog who loves retrieving will be happy to let go of the item.

4. Give him the item again, let it go briefly and hold your hand under his chin immediately. Say "Out" and when he spits it out: 👍.

5. Now place the item in front of your dog on the floor, say "Take it" and "Bring it" and hold your hand calmly in the vicinity.

6. As soon as this works, keep placing the item to be retrieved a bit further away. If it doesn't end up actually in your hand when he brings the item, help by going a bit closer with your hand. Soon you will use 👍 only when he has placed the item in your hand. Only when this works reliably, can you sometimes throw the item.

High Stacking *One more will still work!*

The Task:

Your dog should stack several different objects on top of each other.

For whom? *1 person + 1 dog*

What resources? *Objects to stack*

Requirements? *Retrieving (see page 30f.)*

Step by Step:

1. Take several objects which stack into each other, for example, beakers, cereal bowls, containers. Depending on the shape, this will be easy or difficult for your dog.

2. Give your dog one of the objects and ask him to place it in your hand.

3. Hold this object firmly and give him another one to retrieve.

4. He should now place this on the object in your hand. Keep your hand there initially and hold it in such a way that your dog will find it as easy as possible to guide it into the other object which is already in your hand.

5. From time to time, keep your hand still so your dog has to make more of an effort. If he doesn't quite manage it and the object falls down, encourage him to try again. If it doesn't work out on the second attempt, encourage him again, but this time help him a bit so that it's successful by the third attempt at the latest = 👍.

6. Vary things: it's more difficult with angular objects or a toddler's stacking tower

7. Let your dog stack objects on top of other items instead of in your hand – for example an overturned bowl. This follows the principle of the children's game Jenga, where as many wooden pieces as possible have to be stacked on top of each other and none are allowed to fall down.

◀ **Phoebe** is stacking cereal bowls.

▶ Not so easy – but Mogli can do it really well!

I'm Packing *in my basket*

The Task:

Your dog will learn to clear up his toys and how to carry a small basket.

For whom? 1 person + 1 dog

What resources? Basket, several small objects to retrieve

Requirements? Retrieving (see page 30f.)

Carrying in a basket

First practise just carrying the empty basket. Hold the handle of the basket towards your dog, as shown in the exercise "Mine or Yours?" on page 30f. Then place it in front of you and let him put it in your hand. After this move it one metre away on the floor and ask your dog to bring it to you. Only then practise carrying with the object in the basket.

Step by Step:

1. Start by letting your dog bring an object and place it into your hand = 👍.

2. The next step is to take the small basket into which your dog is to put the objects into one hand.

3. Hold the other hand with your palm facing upwards over the opening of the basket and let him put the object in your hand = 👍.

4. On the next attempt, pull the object slightly to the side at the precise moment when your dog wants to place the item in your hand so that the object falls into the basket = 👍.

5. Soon you will have to hold only the basket towards him instead of your hand and he will put the object into the basket

6. Is it not working out straight away? Perhaps that's because your dog has only recently learned to retrieve and specifically wants to press the object into your hand? It's also possible that he is a bit spooked by the basket to start with. In this case, first practise the exercise "Hide" (see page 64).

7. After he has learned separately to put his nose in the basket when you give the signal "Hide", combine both exercises. Let him retrieve an object and when he's on his way towards you, hold the basket out, say "Hide" and as soon as he puts the object in it, follow with "Out" and 👍.

▶ **This** will also make clearing up fun for your children.

Search & Bring *three dimensional*

The Task:

Pull an object along or down with his paw or teeth using a piece of string.

For whom? *1 person + 1 dog*

What resources? *Object to retrieve, pull toy, thin string*

Requirements? *None*

My dog doesn't tug and therefore doesn't pull on the string. What should I do?

As a preliminary exercise, tie your dog up with a harness on the banister or radiator. Place a small bag filled with desirable food and the string in an arc shape in front of him. This means that when he starts pawing it, he catches the string and can then pull the bag towards him.

Step by Step:

1. This exercise can be a retrieving game but also a mental exercise (see box).
2. First practise the signal "Pull" with your dog.
3. Use an object to do this with which you can play a tugging game.
4. Every time your dog holds the object in his teeth and tries to pull it away, name this behaviour "Pull" and praise him verbally.
5. Say nothing every time you pull the object.
6. If this pulling game goes well, also try it with increasingly thinner pieces of string.
7. Now tie a long thin string onto an object which your dog would like to have – for example onto his favourite toy, a small bag filled with food or a food dummy.
8. Now place this object at a height where your dog can't reach it – only the string which hangs down. For example, on a cupboard, on top of an open door or curtain rail. However, it must match the temperament of your dog because this exercise is not supposed to demolish your home!
9. Hold the string in front of his nose and encourage him by saying "Pull" to pull on it.
10. As soon as the object has fallen down, let him bring it to you and reward him.
11. It's more difficult if he doesn't know where you have hidden the object and he has to search for it and the helpful string in your home.

▲ **Barney** is learning the signal "Pull" without realising it while playing tug.

▼ **Mogli** has found the string. Now he just has to pull it – and the reward will come tumbling down.

Rediscover
Children's Games With Your Dog

Baby toys and lots of children's games are also great for keeping our dogs busy. They encourage motor skills in the same way as they do for toddlers. Everything which small children can grip in their hands, dogs can also take in their mouths. Baby toys should also be free of unhealthy softening agents, but this is not always the case with toys for dogs.

Of course, you don't need to buy everything new. Go to a car boot sale or jumble sale with open eyes, check your shed, attic or garage or ask your friends for children's toys which have been outgrown. You are bound to think of lots of other enjoyable games which you can creatively rediscover with your dog.

Ball Catcher Treat shooting and fetching game

The Task:

Popular children's game, which your dog will also enjoy!

For whom? 1 person + 1 dog
What resources? Ball catcher
Requirements? Retrieving (see page 30f.)

Step by Step:

1. Test whether your dog is frightened of the clicking sound of the "trigger", by first operating it behind your back.
2. Then show him how you put a treat into the beaker and shoot it into the room. He will probably be a bit confused initially, but will soon start to enjoy the game.
3. Aim directly at your dog. It's best if he sits next to you every time.
4. Another option is to let him retrieve a ball and put it in the beaker.
5. Depending on your dog's temperament and preferences, he will then receive a treat as a reward – or you shoot the ball straight away so that he can retrieve it again.
6. Both versions of the game are even more difficult if your ball or treat hunter is only allowed to chase the object he wants when it has already flown through the air, landed and isn't moving. In other words, only when he has sat obediently next to you after you have said "Sit" or "Stay" and waits for your "Okay".
7. **Important:** never let children play this game alone with a dog! And the ball should either be large enough so that your dog can't swallow it or so small that it wouldn't be bad if this happened by accident. This is because large plastic objects which are swallowed could lead to an intestinal obstruction. My border collies really enjoy playing with very small rubber balls, which are only the size of small marbles, and have never swallowed any.

Special version for very intelligent ones!

Place a treat on the floor, which your dog then has to put into the beaker when you say "Bring". Of course, he will then be given it as a reward when it has shot through the air … and after that he can happily finally eat it. It's best to first practise this with a slightly unpopular toy or large biscuit and reward him with sausage out of your hand.

▼ **Even** cautious children really enjoy playing this game as they don't have any contact with the dog's mouth.

Fishing for Ducks *Tails up...*

The Task:

Your dog should fish out floating plastic or rubber animals from a bowl of water.

For whom? *1 person + 1 dog*

What resources? *Floating objects for retrieval, bowl of water*

Requirements? *Retrieving (see page 30f.)*

Step by Step:

1. Let your dog first lift the items from the floor and bring them to you. Reward him for this.

2. Place the object in the bowl which has been filled with a couple of centimetres of water and again ask your dog to bring the item.

3. If this goes well and your dog isn't frightened of the wet water, you can pour increasing amounts of water into the bowl. The higher the water level and the heavier the animals are and therefore the deeper in the water they are floating, the more difficult it becomes. Have you ever tried to fish out an apple from a bowl of water with just your teeth?

Possible variations:

1. Add more ducks or other floating objects.

2. Put a second bowl next to the first and let your dog move the animals from one bowl to the other.

3. Write the numbers 1, 2 or 3 on the ducks. These points mean that your dog will receive 1, 2 or 3 treats as a reward, depending on which duck he brings. Children really enjoy this game.

4. Write various tricks and exercises on the ducks, which your dog must first carry out before receiving a reward.

5. Hide the food between the ducks, after which your dog must search for them. You can buy floating treats and dissolvable ones. Again, start with a couple of centimetres of water in the bowl. Some dogs blow bubbles when they put their mouths under the water.

▶ **These** small ducks can be hunted ...

▼ Tails up!

Letter Mash-up *Scrabble with dogs*

The Task:

Your dog selects several letters with one or both paws, from which you create words.

For whom? 1 person + 1 dog
or several people/children and dogs

What resources? Letter puzzle pieces or several pieces of paper with letters on them

Requirements? Retrieving (see page 30f.) or paw giving (see page 52)

Scrabble for delicate and smart retrievers

You can also play Scrabble with dogs who put things very carefully in their mouths – without needing to practise "Touch" beforehand. Instead of standing on them, encourage the dogs to bring you one letter at a time until every player has the number of letters you have decided beforehand. The person who makes the longest word out of them has won.

Step by Step:

1. Place one of the letters on the palm of your hand and ask your dog to give you a paw. As soon as your dog has touched the letter with his paw = 👍. The new signal which you say from now is "Touch" or "Target" because "Give me a paw" should continue to mean touching your hand with a paw.

2. Then hold the letter with only two fingers in front of him, as soon as he touches the letter with his paw = 👍.

3. Now place the letter just in front of or next to your dog on the floor and say "Touch" encouragingly. At the same time, it's best to put your hands behind your back so that he doesn't confuse these two exercises and looks for your hands. While doing this, don't look in your dog's eyes but rather at the object on the floor. As soon as he touches it with his paw = 👍. If this doesn't work, go back one training step and take the object in your hand again.

4. As soon as your dog enjoys running to letters which are further away and touches them briefly = 👍. If he wants to come directly to you afterwards to collect his reward, first guide him back to the letter with the promised treat until he at least puts his paw on it calmly and only then let go of the treat.

5. While he is quietly still chewing, give him another 👍 and repeat the word "Touch". This is how he will understand over time that when you have sent him to a field containing several letters with "Touch" again later, he should stand calmly on one letter ("Target") and wait there until 👍 and the reward comes.

▶ "I'll take a U!"

Stacking Rings — *Ring throwing game & ring pyramid*

The Task:

Your dog is allowed to retrieve rings and place them on a ring throwing game or pyramid.

For whom? *1 person + 1 dog*

What resources? *Ring throwing game, ring pyramid, or diving rings & a wooden rod*

Requirements? *Retrieving (see page 30f.)*

Step by Step:

1. Take an individual rod from the game in your hand and encourage your dog to retrieve a ring. If he then comes towards you with it, thread the ring through the rod with a skilful movement of your hand and say "Out". As soon as the ring touches your wrist = 👍. Give this exercise a name, for example "Place".

2. After a few repetitions, put the rod into one end of the two halves of the game and hold them near the rod firmly in your hand. Initially your dog will look close to your hand and want to put the ring down there.

3. It's easier for him if you first hold the game in front of you, then later like an extended arm to your side. Every time your dog touches the rod = 👍.

4. If the ring falls on the floor, encourage him with "Bring" and "Place" to try again – help him on the second or third attempt a bit by moving the rod towards him. As soon as the ring is hanging = 👍.

Version for fusspots

Ring pyramids for babies and toddlers can also be used. Depending on the type of pyramid, the rings and their internal diameter become increasingly smaller and the game more difficult. Give your dog the next ring in the sequence. Your dog now has to be very skilful so that it works, particularly when the rings have to be placed on top of each other horizontally and precisely.

5. Build the game up into a cross and kneel on the floor with it. Let your ring juggler retrieve again, don't look into his eyes, but at the game in front of you. Help him less and less.

6. Now place the game on the floor and continually further away from you. Point in the direction of the game or briefly hold your hand close to a rod. Say "Place" and "Out" and pull your hand to the side so that the ring slips onto the rod.

▼ Mogli is trying to bring the ring as close to your hand as possible.

Playing Football *Score a GOAL!*

The Task:

Dribbling in the sitting room – your dog pushes a ball into a goal with his nose.

For whom? *1 person + 1 dog*

What resources? *1 ball and 1 goal or target*

Requirements? *None*

▲ Nudge. "Is this right?"

Step by Step:

1. Hold a ball in front of your dog's nose – this can be a child's football or a small gymnastics ball. It should be a ball which has so far not been used for retrieving. This is because in that case he is likely to try to take the ball into his mouth. If applicable select a larger ball.

2. Reaffirm the first sign of interest, even if it's just a glance in the direction of the ball and not even a touch = 👍.

3. Now every so often require a bit more activity from your dog and reaffirm every action in the right direction with = 👍. This also includes approaching, sniffing, touching and increasingly firmer nudging. Every time describe this with the new signal "Nudge".

4. If this becomes increasingly reliable and in response to your signal, then place the ball in front of your dog on the floor. Every nudge is again followed by = 👍.

5. In the next exercise don't immediately give reaffirmation after the first nudge, but rather wait a moment while looking at the ball and encourage your dog to touch the ball a second time with "Nudge". Only then is this followed by = 👍.

6. Now give reaffirmation to your dog at irregular intervals, sometimes even after two or three consecutive nudges or after a particularly firm nudge.

7. Then place the ball just in front of a goal or another easily visible target. As soon as he pushes the ball into this, show huge enjoyment and shout "GOAL!" Of course, give a particularly nice reward. Gradually increase the distance.

▲ Molly rolls an empty feed ball into the GOAL!

What to do if it doesn't work immediately?

Does your dog not have a clue and simply doesn't nudge the ball? Then place the ball onto a small feeding bowl in which he can see that you have placed a treat and put the ball on top of it.

All Kinds of Tricks

In this chapter everything focuses on tricks for the sitting room. It includes popular traditional ones and various versions of them, easy and enjoyable ones but also a few difficult tricks, which you will have to practise for a while. For most of them you don't need anything other than your dog, a few treats and a good mood.

What's the point of all this you might ask? You dog really doesn't care whether you use the commands "Sit", "Stay" and "Come" or "Give a paw" and teach him the role. It doesn't matter to him. But it does to us! When practising tricks, we are usually far more relaxed and also occasionally smile if something doesn't work instantly. This is how your dog learns much faster and more enjoyably, as you will see. Practise "Sit" and "Stay" calmly in this way as if it's only a trick!

Hello! *Giving a paw*

The Task:

The most traditional trick, which people who don't have a dog also enjoy.

For whom? 1 person + 1 dog
What resources? None
Requirements? None

Doesn't your dog want to lift his paw?

Scratch him on the back of his paw, tickle his toes or in between them or push a finger to the side under the ball of his paw. Place your hand on top of his toes and then press them lightly to the floor. This will be a bit unpleasant so that he will then lift his paw of his own accord.

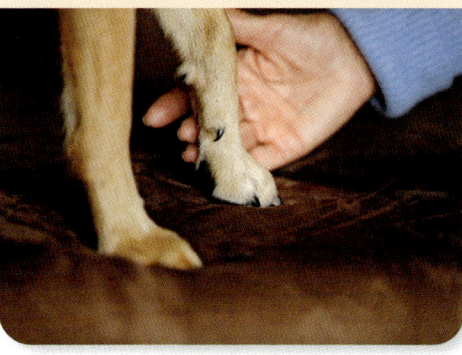

Step by Step:

1. Kneel down in front of your sitting dog. Place the rewards behind or next to you on a table so that your hands are empty. Only grab them after your 👍.

2. Stroke your dog with your fingers along his leg. Dogs are often ticklish and will therefore pull their paws away.

3. At the very moment when your dog briefly lifts his paw from the floor: 👍.

4. The next time try to have contact for a second with the ball of his paw by skilfully turning your hand with an open palm = 👍.

5. Repeat all this several times with the aim of maintaining contact for a bit longer every time by following the movement of his paws. 👍

6. Try to give him the treat as quickly as possible after 👍 while his paw is still resting on your hand, but don't hold it.

7. As soon as your dog has his treat and is chewing, he will hold his paw more calmly.

8. Soon he will leave it for longer and more happily on your hand and wait for 👍. Start casually repeatedly saying your new signal for paw giving.

9. Now only hold your hand close to his paw and say your signal. Wait a moment to see whether he is able to have the right idea himself. If necessary, help him a bit and touch his leg lightly with your finger.

10. It won't take long before he lifts his paw on his own as soon as your hand approaches.

11. Does he place it in your hand the first time? Bingo!

▶ "Hello! Can I have a biscuit now?"

High Five ... and bye-bye

The Task:

Lifting his paws higher than for giving paw and hitting your hand to say "High five" and then waving or saying "Bye-bye".

For whom? *1 person + 1 dog*

What resources? *None*

Requirements? *Giving paw (see page 52)*

Step by Step:

So far, your dog "gives paw" when your palm and fingertips face downwards. For "High five" your hand should also touch his paw when you point your fingertips upwards. However, for many people this means "Stop", "Wait" or "Stay". Therefore, your dog will probably not do this instantly – even if you say the signal "Paw" which he has learned in the meantime. He will still learn really quickly with a little trick.

1. Imagine a clock face. At the start your fingertips face downwards when you say "Paw", just like previously at six o'clock.

2. The next time when you hold your hand out, turn them slightly so that your fingertips now show five o'clock, then four o'clock, three o'clock, etc.

3. As soon as this works when your fingertips are facing upwards, start your new sign, for example "High five" 👍.

4. Mark the moment when his paw meets your hand at the top increasingly precisely. This is how he will soon link your hand and the word signal.

5. As soon as your dog is confident with "High five", you can create another trick from this: namely waving. Here your dog should learn to wave one of his paws around in the air in response to an appropriate hand gesture such as opening and closing your fingers, a movement of your hand to and fro or the word signal "Bye-bye".

▲ "We did that really well. High five!"

▶ **Nice dog.** Mogli always says goodbye really politely.

"Wave bye-bye!"

Now pull your hand away just before your dog can touch you with his paw and then hold it back out again so that he first touches thin air and then waves it around again = 👍. Really precise timing is very important so that he understands as quickly as possible that it's now about waving his paw in thin air and no longer touching your hand.

High Ten *Double high five*

The Task:

With the "High ten" trick, your dog will stand on his hind legs and touch your hands with both his front paws.

For whom? 1 person + 1 dog
What resources? None
Requirements? High five (see page 54)

Tips & Tricks

It's a bit more difficult to work with the clicker here as you need both hands for the exercise. However, you can use a button clicker, which you operate with your teeth or can place under your foot so that you can click it. Or use a click word. Another alternative would be to ask a helper to click for you at the right time.

Step by Step:

1. Once again start with the "High five" trick, only this time continuously delay 👍. By doing this, you are reaffirming and rewarding your dog for keeping his paw in your hand for continually longer periods of time.

2. If your dog pulls his paw away too early, say "Shame" sadly – and encourage him to try again. Reaffirm and reward him a bit earlier the next time.

3. Now your dog must also learn how to "stick" his paw to your hand when you move it to the right, left, down or up or put pressure on it. Don't forget 👍 !

4. If you continually move your hand further up and your paw artist can keep his paw there, at some point his other front paw will lose contact with the floor. Use this instant to skilfully place your other hand under this paw and give him an opportunity to support himself on it, which he will gratefully accept. Also don't forget 👍 .

5. If he doesn't allow you to press against his paw, briefly touch his lower leg with your other hand and say "Paw" encouragingly. Then hold your other hand next to it and continually slightly higher until he is looking for your hands of his own accord with both paws as soon as you have both of them at the same height in front of him.

6. The new signal for this trick could be called "High ten". Or clap your hands before you start each time before he gives the high ten.

7. Stand up gradually until you can stand in front of your dog – depending on the size of your dog and he goes up on his hind legs to be able to reach your hands.

▶ "Who is taller: you or me?"

All Good Things Come in Threes Roll & Co.

The Task:

Your dog learns to roll on his side. On his way to doing this, he will also learn two additional tricks ...

For whom? 1 person + 1 dog
What resources? None
Requirements? Giving paw (see page 52)

Perhaps you have already tried to teach your dog how to roll by using food to tempt him? Most dogs become a bit agitated through this and just try to reach the treat somehow. And if the enticing hand isn't there, they won't roll over again.

In the way described here, your dog will learn how to develop body awareness, roll over slowly and deliberately without turning his back. The best thing on the way to doing this, is that you can teach him two other great tricks:

"Go to sleep" and "Hands up". This is because once your dog can "roll", it becomes more difficult to teach him that he should stop again after a quarter- or half-turn.

▲ **Reward** always only when your dog's head is lying on the floor.

Step by Step: "Sleep"

1. Sit down next to your dog on the floor – preferably when he is already tired and would like to lie down anyway.

2. If he is lying down in his usual "place", then stroke him on his side and stomach until he rolls over on his side and is relaxed.

3. Continue stroking, but at the beginning don't give any treats! Otherwise, he will probably want to jump up again. Simply say a word of praise very quietly and your new signal "Sleep".

4. Then quietly reach for a treat. If he lifts his head, say "Sleep" again. If he doesn't lay it back down, guide his head with the treat in front of his nose back down to the floor and only give it then. He will soon understand.

▲ Giving paw lying down.

▲ "Hands up" – and the roll is almost there.

Step by Step: "Hands up"

1. If your dog now lays down on his side as you want in response to your signal "Sleep" and stays lying quietly, encourage him to give you his paw while lying down.

2. Where is his paw flailing in the air? Hold your hand close to it so that he can touch it. It's not so easy for him to coordinate this while lying down.

3. Now hold your hand a few centimetres higher every time. Always when he reaches it = 👍, until he is lying completely on his back, touches your hand above him and has learned how to balance. As a word signal for this say "Hands up".

4. Then hold your hand slightly higher until he can no longer reach it. Reassure him when he stretches his paws upwards and remains lying quietly like this.

Step by Step: the "Roll"

1. The roll is almost there. The important thing is that if your dog has sometimes lost his balance when practising "Hands up" and already completed the roll, you have not already rewarded this. Otherwise, he will be confused when learning "Hands up".

2. As soon as the signal for "Hands up" has been absorbed after a few days, you can let your dog "Sleep" again. Then encourage him once more with a movement of your hand to "Hands up". This time make a slightly more swinging movement so that he rolls beyond the stationary point and lands with his paws on the other side.

3. And there it is: the roll! Cheerfully reward him and always say the new signal "Roll" when you are practising the exercise again.

Let's Jump! *Through my arms*

The Task:

Your dog will learn to jump through your arms as soon as you form a circle with them and say "Jump".

For whom? 2 people + 1 dog
What resources? None
Requirements? None

Tips & Tricks

Does your dog cheat his way past your arms? Ask your helper to stand very close to your arms. You can cover the empty space under your arms with a towel or blanket and also slightly increase the space between your arms at the beginning. Now your high jumper has no alternative but to jump through your arms.

Step by Step:

1. It looks best if your dog jumps through your arms from behind and you are both facing in the same direction.

2. Wash your hands so that they don't smell of food and your dog doesn't sniff them. Initially he will only receive rewards from your helper.

3. Stand or kneel in your position and ask your helper to entice your dog with a treat by holding it front of your arms. He doesn't have to jump yet – climbing through also counts.

4. As soon as all four paws have passed through the circle of your arms, your helper should lead your dog with the treat in front of his nose in an arc back around to the starting position and only let go of it there. This means that your dog is already back in the right place to repeat the exercise.

5. Give him the visual signal for "Sit" and again place yourself with your arms in a circle right in front of him and say "Jump". Your helper should again give you some assistance and immediately try to see whether your dog already follows his hand gesture and jumps through your arms when there is obviously no longer a treat in your hands. In this way he will consciously be aware of the circle made by your arms and will soon jump of his own accord, instead of only chasing after the treat.

6. From now on your helper should have the reward in the other hand, holding it and enticing your dog back to the starting position after a successful jump.

7. From time to time your helper should wait slightly longer after you say "Jump" and make increasingly smaller hand gestures until your dog already jumps through your arms on your signal.

▲ Milo licks the sausage and is skilfully led back to the start.

▶ Perfect!

Feet *Right in the middle instead of nearby!*

The Task:

Your dog should walk between the person's legs and stand on their feet to walk with them.

For whom? *1 person + 1 dog*
What resources? *None*
Requirements? *None*

Step by Step:

1. Entice your dog to go between your legs with a treat from behind: 👍.

2. With another treat in front of his nose, entice him in slow motion very slowly in a small arc around your leg. With smaller dogs you can turn your toes inwards in the front and slowly entice them forwards.

3. Some dogs might accidentally put a paw on your foot: 👍.

4. If you have enticed him too far or he has put his paws beyond your foot, then lead your hand back in the direction of your belly over his head very slowly upwards. He will reach and stretch and might land on your foot: 👍.

5. If his paw moves away forwards, say "Shame" and start all over again.

6. At the beginning call one side "Fee", the other "t". Also try to make both paws stand on your feet one after the other. Help by keeping your feet close together next to or behind his paws so it's easier.

7. Now he must wait longer every now and then 👍. Hold the treat at the level of your tummy button in your open palm above it, later your hand will be empty. Always give him the food with the other hand which is otherwise behind your back – because food in front of his nose is a distraction.

8. This is how he will stand on your feet of his own accord from the middle position, when you say "Feet".

▶ **It's already working well!** Now Tilly can start to take small steps until it looks like the photo on page 51.

▲ **Pearl** is enticed very slowly forwards and backwards in slow motion.

Hide *What does the ostrich do?*

The Task:

On the signal "Hide" your dog should put his nose into a container and keep it there briefly.

For whom? *1 person + 1 dog*

What resources? *Small basket, cone, etc.*

Requirements? *None*

Step by Step:

1. Let your dog see you put a treat into a suitable container.

2. Hold the container out. When he puts his nose in to reach for the treat, describe this behaviour with 👍 and also say your future signal – for example "Hide".

3. Let him sit and wait while you hide a treat in the container. Then encourage him with "Hide" to fetch it. Always at the precise time his nose disappears into the container: 👍. After he has dived in, give him another treat from your hand.

4. The next few times pretend that you have hidden something, give your signal and as soon as his nose dives in: 👍. From now on there will be a treat from your hand only after this has been done.

5. Now don't reassure him immediately after the first time, but encourage him to put his nose in the container again with "Hide". Only then will there be 👍.

Important!

If your children practise "Hide" with your dog, then make sure they only do this with items where your dog's head won't get stuck. The items should also be made of materials which are not airtight so that he can still breathe. Otherwise drill a hole into the top of the container just to be safe.

6. With the next sequences of exercises always reassure him when his nose remains in the container for a bit longer than previously. This will mean he holds the position continuously longer over time.

7. **Different version:** if you now hide the container under a sand-coloured blanket and instead of saying "Hide" to your dog, as a signal, ask "What does the ostrich do?", you have a new amusing version to make your audience laugh.

▶ One, two, three, hide. My nose must be hidden.

Skateboarding *Taking the dog for a walk is so yesterday...*

For whom? *1 person + 1 dog*

What resources? *Skateboard*

Requirements? *Giving paw (see page 52)*

The Task:

Your dog should learn how to stand on a skateboard and travel on it. If you simply place the skateboard in front of your dog and encourage him to touch it with his paws, he will usually start to paw at it and the skateboard then begins to move backwards instead of him pushing it forwards.

With a little trick, you can stop it even going so far. First ask him to give the traditional paw: 👍. Then place the skateboard on your lower arm and keep your other hand on the board. Now ask him to give paw again. If your dog now places his paws on the hand resting on the board: 👍.

The next time pull your hand away just before the paw touches your hand so that the paw now touches the skateboard: 👍.

Name the moment the paw touches the board with a new signal, for example "Skate" because if you continue saying "Paw", it will confuse your dog as "Paw" has so far meant touching your hands – and it should remain that way.

Step by Step:

1. Now hold the skateboard out towards your future racing driver and say your new signal "Skate". If he lifts his paw immediately and touches the board: 👍. Otherwise help him again with a small hand gesture. After a few repetitions he will immediately touch the skateboard with his paw on your signal "Skate".

2. Now place the skateboard in front of him on the floor and say your signal again.

3. If he also touches it there with his paw: 👍.

4. But make sure that you never reaffirm him if he has pulled the board towards him. He must learn to push it forwards to ride it. This usually happens automatically when the movement makes your dog place a paw on the skateboard.

5. During the next step let your dog sit one to two metres away and wait, tap your hand on the surface of the skateboard right in front of his face and then place it back on the floor.

6. Go to him and stand next to him.

7. Put your hands behind your back so they don't distract him from the skateboard.

8. Don't look at him, but look forwards at the skateboard. Go slowly with him towards the skateboard and just before he reaches it say "Skate" encouragingly. As soon as he touches it and it rolls forward the first few centimetres, praise him precisely at the time when he is briefly riding on it: 👍.

9. Now continually delay 👍 so that he goes on the skateboard again and continues to push it.

▼ "And when I'm grown up, I'm going to be a racing driver!"

Back up *The handstand*

The Task:

Your dog will learn how to intentionally climb on objects backwards with his hind paws.

For whom? *1 person + 1 dog*

What resources? *Thick books, boards, a sturdy box/crate*

Requirements? *None*

▲ **Merlin** had to practise a lot until a handstand was this good.

Step by Step:

1. Place a long board or large book on the floor.

2. Lead your dog with a hand gesture or a treat forwards over the obstacle. As soon as he is standing with his front paws back on the floor with his hind paws still on the object, stop him: 👍.

3. Guide your dog upwards again and if he again stands on the object using only his hind paws, say your new signal – for example "Back up". Repeat your signal and 👍 several times.

4. Encourage him to move a few centimetres further forwards, for example to briefly touch your hand with his nose so that his hind paws briefly come to a halt just before the obstacle. **Important:** if possible, don't entice him with a treat to get down. A reward will be given only when he stands with his hind legs up.

5. Say "Back up" and wait briefly to see whether he already tries to go up backwards again: if not, lead him into an arc, again approaching from the back and 👍, when he is standing correctly.

6. If he reacts reliably to "Back up", then increase the number of items every day for him to climb on. It can take a while until his back paws are this coordinated and he can do it without any help. Lots of dogs initially have no feeling for their hindquarters.

7. Over time this will also work on the edge of the sofa, a wide box/crate or a chair against a wall. Help him with a hand gesture to always position himself initially at a right angle to the object before you encourage him to "Back up".

◀ Sandy nudges my hand and looks for the book again with her hind legs.

▶ Your sofa is perfect for more practice.

Your Dog as Your Helper

Do you sometimes wish you had some help around the house? Then why don't you simply teach your dog some new tricks? Most dogs really enjoy having a job to do and one can see how proud they are when they have done something well.

For example, teach your dog how to collect old socks which are lying around and put them in a laundry basket or put them over a low washing line. If you have already practised the exercises "Mine or Yours?" (page 30f.) and "I'm packing in my basket" (page 34), then this will be child's play!

You can find other amusing suggestions in the following chapter.

Have fun practising!

A Visitor? *Quickly roll out the red carpet!*

The Task:

In future your dog will roll out the red carpet for visitors and give them a great welcome.

For whom? *1 person + 1 dog*

What resources? *Small rug or similar*

Requirements? *None*

What do I do now?

From time to time put fewer or no treats in the rolled-up rug. Your dog will receive a reward from you as soon as he has completely unrolled the rug. Or let your dog make another trick out of rolling it back up and the visitor can hand over the reward. Your dog and your guest will enjoy this!

Step by Step:

1. Take a small rug, a bath mat or a table mat for very small dogs.

2. Your dog should now wait and watch you. If he is too curious and finds it difficult to wait, tie him to a fixed object with a lead or ask a helper to hold him.

3. Kneel down in front of him and let him watch how you roll up the rug and hide a treat inside every few centimetres. You can make this exciting by saying: "Oohh, look what I've got here …"

4. Leave about ten centimetres of the carpet unrolled and place a treat on it. This will make it easier for your dog at the start.

5. Lots of dogs quickly begin to paw at the carpet to reach the treat more quickly and crumple up the rug if you're not careful. Therefore, you should kneel opposite him and wave your hands to the right and left over the ends of the rug. This means that if he tries to paw at it, you can quickly hold the rug and make him understand that he should try something different. If you have a very impetuous dog, maybe someone could additionally put a brake on him from the back on the lead.

6. If he already knows the "Nudge" signal (see page 48), you can also help him verbally if he always wants to use his paws.

▲ Rona will soon also be rolling out larger rugs enthusiastically.

Oh, it's Dark in Here ... *I need some light!*

The Task:

In response to the signal "Light" your dog will activate a switch and switch the light on or off.

For whom? *1 person + 1 dog*

What resources? *Lamp with a foot switch*

Requirements? *Giving paw (see page 52)*

What should I do if it doesn't work?

Avoid looking at your dog expectantly, but instead look at the switch on the floor. Usually, he will follow your gaze. Don't also help him by pointing to the switch. Most dogs will then be irritated and won't know whether they should touch the switch or your hand. It's therefore best to place your hands behind your back.

Step by Step:

1. Ask your dog to refresh the traditional paw giving: 👍.

2. Take the switch in your hand as shown in the photo on page 75 and ask him to give you his paw again.

3. Every time your dog touches the switch with his paw: 👍.

4. If possible, try to give him the treat when his paw is on the switch in your hand. He will then link the reward more quickly with touching the switch.

5. Soon he will lift his paw as soon as you reach towards the switch with your hand, also without you needing to say your previous signal of "Give paw". This is the time when you introduce the new signal – for example "Light".

6. Now hold your dog and your hand with the switch a bit lower every time. Whenever he touches the switch with his paw, you say "Light" and reaffirm him with 👍.

7. For the rest of the exercise, you say "Light" just before or while he is lifting his paw – in other words before he has touched the switch.

8. Now place the switch on the floor in front of your dog and say "Light" encouragingly.

9. When your dog briefly touches the switch with his paw: 👍. If the light comes on while this is happening = jackpot!

▶ "I think I've just had a lightbulb moment!"

"Take it" *Hold it tightly*

The Task:

Your dog should hold an umbrella or broom handle by putting his paw around it.

For whom? *1 person + 1 dog*
What resources? *Umbrella or broom handle*
Requirements? *Giving paw (see page 52)*

Step by Step:

1. Prepare your dog for the forthcoming exercise by again starting with the traditional paw giving.
2. The next step is to take an umbrella or broom handle and hold it diagonally in front of him. Hold one of your hands over it and ask him to give paw again. As soon as your dog touches your hand lying on the umbrella with his paw: 👍.
3. During one of the next repetitions, pull your hand away just before he touches it so that he is touching the umbrella instead: 👍.
4. Your dog will soon lift his paw of his own accord when you hold out the umbrella again. Now be careful to ensure that he doesn't only touch the umbrella but, if possible, hangs his paw over it. You can help this by moving the umbrella in his direction.
5. Now introduce a new signal – for example "Take it" or "Hold tight".
6. Now guide the umbrella a bit higher every time and reaffirm your dog only when he places his paw around the umbrella and not when he merely touches it. This is because he should later grasp the umbrella and not push his paw away.
7. It will take a while until he grasps the umbrella and holds it as you want him to – even if it is standing right next to him. This is because it's a very untypical movement for a dog. Give him time to understand what you would like him to do.

▲ **Slowly** move the umbrella more and more upright. Reaffirm only when his paw is already grasping the umbrella.

▶ **Barney** with brolly and charm – but without a bowler hat.

Training tip

Your dog must learn to push his head against the umbrella so that it doesn't fall over. It's therefore best to start with a preliminary exercise. When you want to unexpectedly nudge a dog or person to the side, they usually push against you with a reflex action. So, lean the umbrella against your dog's neck: 👍. Practice with more pressure from time to time until your dog leans against the umbrella: 👍.

On Your Socks *get set, go…*

For whom? *1 person + 1 dog*

What resources? *Socks and washing line*

Requirements? *Retrieving (see page 30f.)*

The Task:

I'm sure you have some odd socks in your sock drawer, don't you? Well now you finally have a sensible way of using them! You can keep your dog occupied for hours with these socks and even study entire behaviour chains.

The exercise on page 34 explains how to teach your dog to place items in a basket. You can practise placing socks in a laundry basket in the same way. Here you will learn how to teach your dog to hang socks on a line and on the following two pages your dog will learn how to pull your socks off and bring clean ones from the drawer.

You can combine the individual exercises as you wish into behaviour chains at the end. Your dog will then have to complete several individual exercises one after the other and will only receive a reward at the very end. First always practise the last partial step in the chain and reassure him with 👍. Now and then set another partial step at the beginning and give a reward as soon as both tasks have been completed. For example, like this: taking the socks out of the washing machine and putting them in the basket. Or taking the socks out of the laundry basket and hanging them on the line.

Step by Step:

1. Place one sock on the floor and make your dog practise putting it in your hand: 👍.

2. Erect a washing line at the chest height of your dog. For example, you could fasten the dog lead to a table leg and hold the other end with your hand.

3. Let your dog bring you another sock and now hold your empty hand directly over the line. Just before he places the sock in your hand, pull it back a bit so that the sock lands on the washing line: 👍.

4. If the sock lands next to it the first time, still reward him.

5. If the sock falls down again the next time, then encourage him with "Bring" to try again and this time hold your hand directly under the line. Is it hanging this time? Great and 👍!

6. Do you have the feeling that over time your dog has now understood what this is about, but is often overexcited and throws the sock around? Then try to approach the exercise more calmly and go back a learning step.

7. Your dog should be successful by the second or third attempt at the latest and receive a reward from you so that he doesn't lose his enjoyment of the game. Help him a bit, if necessary, by holding out your hand or moving it towards him as appropriate.

8. Soon he will hang the socks "tidily" over the washing line.

▼ The good ones on the washing line, the bad ones … in the laundry basket.

Socks Off!

The Task:

Your dog learns the signal "Pull" and can therefore be helpful to you.

For whom? *1 person + 1 dog*

What resources? *Tug toy, thin string, old socks*

Requirements? *Signal "Pull" (see page 36)*

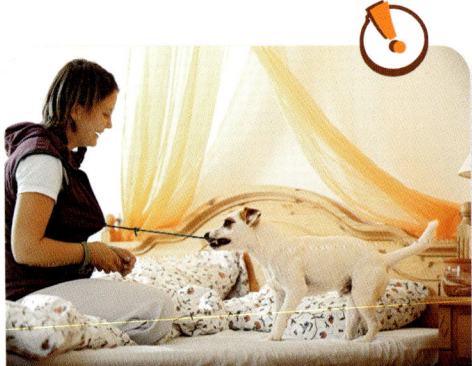

More tasks for your butler

"Pulling" games are very easy to combine with retrieving games. Show your dog how to put a pair of socks into the drawer. Now encourage him to bring a pair of socks to your bed after you have pulled the drawer open (see page 30f.). Or let him put the socks into the laundry basket after you have taken them off (see page 78).

Step by Step:

1. Practise pulling again in response to the signal, by letting your dog tug and/or pull on a piece of string.

2. Then tie the string to the handle of a drawer and hold the end of the string in front of him with the request "Take it" or "Pull". As soon as he has his teeth on it or even pulls it: 👍.

3. It might help to choose a drawer which is almost at floor level and hide a favourite toy or treat in it in front of your dog. Then the incentive and therefore the likelihood are greater that he will make more of an effort.

4. **Important:** practise with one drawer in which there is usually nothing interesting or exciting for your dog so that he will not try it on his own at any time. He is only allowed to pull drawers open when a piece of string is tied to them and you tell him to do so.

5. Now take an old, single sock, with which you play a tugging game, while saying "Pull" and sometimes let your dog win. Pull a sock over your fist and say "Pull" again. If he then touches your hand with his teeth, briefly squeal so that he takes more care in the future because it would hurt your toes later on.

6. After he has carefully pulled the sock off your fist, you can put it over your foot. Initially only over your toes and later over your entire foot and then your dog should pull the sock off.

7. If both exercises work well, your dog will also quickly learn how to pull up a zip and to take off your jacket by pulling on the ends of the sleeves.

▶ **Ready**, steady, PULL!

Messenger Service *"You have post"*

The Task:

Your dog plays postman and brings you or family members messages.

For whom? *1 or more people + 1 dog*

What resources? *Short messages, shoebox or postbox*

Requirements? *None – if applicable, retrieving (see page 30f.)*

This is great fun – not only for children. If your dog is a very delicate and careful retriever, he can carry rolled-up paper in his mouth and give it to you. On the other hand, if your dog is very boisterous and tends to chew objects, then you can pack up the messages in something more robust, which is easy for him to carry. If he really doesn't like retrieving, then simply tie the message to his collar. The recipient of the message then calls the four-legged postman over by his name.

Step by Step:

1. The message can either be handed over to your dog by a family member and then brought to you.
2. But you can also put the message in a shoebox or a different "letter box" and let him bring it from there.
3. Gradually increase the level of difficulty.
4. First put the open letter box very close to you on the floor and let your dog bring you a roll of paper or an envelope from there.
5. Your signal for this could be "Bring the post".
6. Close the letter box or shoebox a little bit further every time until your dog has learned to open it on his own and to retrieve the message.
7. Now you can move further and further away from the letter box until your dog brings you the message from a different room or floor.

The post has arrived …

A new version is to install a letter box in your home. It could also be an old bread bin, which was going to be thrown out. Your dog can force it open from the front with his nose. It also works with a shoebox where your dog can lift the lid. Or the modern alternative: an American letter box. Your dog can open the flap with a piece of string (see pages 36 and 80).

▶ Chinese whispers … almost.

Games to Play Outside

Let's go Outside!

The highlights of our dogs' lives are the daily walks, as well as feeding times. Every healthy dog loves being outside. Above all, a dog's nose longs for variety and keeping busy – our dogs really need this routine. We dog owners also enjoy being out and about. This is part of having a dog and is also relaxing, healthy, and sometimes extremely entertaining.

Active and Happy

Nevertheless, there are ways of increasing all this. I promise you that games to keep busy will not only be fun for your dog, but also for you! Having an attentive, laughing companion at your side, will also make you smile. Playing games which are educational and fun with your dog are self-rewarding – for the animal and the owner. At the same time, the connection between you will grow, not only that from the dog to his owner, but also vice versa. You will be proud of your four-legged friend and this will also be enjoyable for him. And this is how going for a walk becomes the highlight of the day, not a real chore! In this book I will show you lots of options to increase the entertainment value of your daily round trip. The effort required is usually low – and yet it will bring so much enjoyment! It's not about entertaining your dog from start to finish, but two to three different activities on every walk will enrich his life tremendously. With a slight change to the usual expression: "If your dog is happy, the owner is happy!"

Biscuits Instead of Pressure

The great thing about your active walk will be that there is no pressure for it to be successful because playing is by definition without a purpose. We don't have to pass any exams. There is no competition, just enjoyment of each other, which guarantees the fun factor. Nevertheless, successful experiences are also important for you and your dog.

Apart from patience, you don't really need many "tools" to achieve this. Using a clicker or a special word of praise (marker signal, see page 90), will already help a lot with learning. Also find out how your hand or an object can become a "dog magnet"

▶ The aim is to have fun together!

(also known as a target, see page 92). Of course, the most important thing for your dog is to give frequent, generous rewards because even small steps are a reason for lots of enjoyment! A wide variety of rewards is particularly effective. Find out what your pet regards as a reward and what is appropriate for the relevant situation. For many dogs, food is the most popular reward. This is good news because treats are easy and fast to provide. For example, you can use various different food bags which are loosely attached to your clothing to take with you. I always have food for my dogs at two value levels with me: one is a good dry food as well as sausage or cheese.

However, there are lots of other options: your jubilant voice, a great game of tug, throwing a ball, also freedom to sniff or playing with your canine friend. Your dog will enjoy variety and surprises. Please be very generous with your praise and rewards! Observe yourself and count how often you give your dog positive reinforcement. He will be happy to repeat things if they are worth the effort for him. Therefore, when you see good behaviour, reward it: sometimes only with a friendly word, sometimes with high-value food or a cheerful ball game. We really don't want to be one of those people whose motto is "Silence is praise enough!" Sometimes I'm asked: "Are you never going to feed him again?" My answer is a very clear "Yes, why ever not!" Why shouldn't I take this opportunity to give my dog a reward, when it's so easy and he enjoys it so much? An animal which is "disciplined" goes through the world more cautiously and is more mistrustful.

A dog given frequent rewards is a more attentive and cheerful companion. If there's a choice between pressure or a biscuit, I will choose the biscuit. I wish you and your dog lots of great outdoor experiences and fun together!

At a glance

How difficult is it to put the idea into practice? Does it also work with several dogs or on the lead? You will find this information for every set of instructions.

With or without a lead?

 Only possible off the lead (free)

 With the lead

With how many dogs?

 Only possible with one dog

 Possible with several dogs

How difficult?

 Easy

 Medium

 Challenging

Practical Information
for Your Dog Walk

Your dog doesn't mind whether you are playing just for fun or whether your aim is to have a well-mannered companion. He wants variety, attention, delicious rewards and lots of fun! You can really use the daily walks to combine both these things …

You can look forward to interesting walks and you will benefit from joint activities and a strengthened connection.

Ignore Joggers *and identify strange(rs)/things calmly*

What resources? None
Requirements? None

The Task:

Your dog will learn about which people or objects might threaten him while you are on a walk and how to stay calm.

It can be helpful for young dogs and less confident ones to deal with environmental stimuli better if we give them a name. For example, if we see a jogger in front of the dog, we can point them out (see box) and he will be less surprised when they suddenly appear. In addition, he will link the trigger positively from the outset because it is associated with a marker signal and a reward.

Lots of undesired behaviour by our dogs is based on fear. Joggers are barked at because they appear threatening. Likewise with horses and other dogs. Giving something a name helps our animal companions to classify something unknown. Fearful situations such as thunder can also be named and become more bearable through positive conditioning.

The game also has a favourable side effect: in this way dogs learn an impressive vocabulary!

Step by Step:

From the time they are puppies, I teach my dogs the words "Jogger", "Bicycle", "Car", "Children", "Horse", "Dog", etc. The first glance at the assumed danger is marked and rewarded:

1. As soon as a possible stimulus trigger comes into their field of vision, point it out: "Look, a jogger!" You name the object and give a marker signal so that your dog also notices it.

2. If the body language of your dog indicates that he has seen the jogger – which could be a glance in that direction, a twitch of the ear or something similar – reward him.

3. If your dog starts to turn to you expecting a marker signal on identifying a jogger, you can build up alternative behaviour and reward it, for example eye contact with him.

Tip from a professional:

For example, if your dog is familiar with sheep and horses and if both are visible, you can "practise vocabulary". Name the sheep and give a reward when your dog then looks in that direction. Say "Horse!" and give a reward if he looks over at the horse!

What is a marker signal?

A marker signal tells your dog precisely: "That's correct!" It's a promise of a reward. Marker signals can be the clicking of a clicker but also words such as "Yep!", "Chop-chop!" or a click of the tongue. Give various generous rewards for anything your dog enjoys.

▶ A jogger is coming? Great, that means a treat!

Stay Cool   Walk on the right or left

What resources? None
Requirements? None

The Task:

Even in places where our dogs are allowed to run freely, we are not the only ones who are outside. We will encounter other pedestrians, joggers and cyclists and it's very helpful if your dog stays obediently by your side even when not wearing a lead.

In contrast to the training ground, it's not about walking correctly here. Instead, your four-legged companion will learn how to reliably ignore distractions.

Target stick

A target stick as an extension of your arm might be useful with smaller dogs. Instead of always having to bring a target stick you have bought in a shop, you can make one yourself while you are out: simply fasten a handkerchief onto a stick with a hair tie! Now your dog only has to learn how to follow it.

Step by Step:

1. Start on a wide path. When you see someone coming towards you, point them out to your dog. Put him on a lead, hold it in your left hand and guide him with a treat to your right side past the distraction. Shortly after the encounter, click and reward.

2. Very soon the treat in your hand will be replaced by a hand target (see page 106). You want your dog to go past the person, guided by your empty right hand. It will help him if there is a task: following your hand.

3. Another form of assistance is to walk very obviously on the right. This will then become a signal for your dog to go onto the right edge of the path next to you. It then becomes clear to the approaching walker that the dog is under control.

4. It's therefore a progression from naming – an alternative task is the hand target – rewarding shortly after the encounter. Make sure that you give the reward to the right of you. Although the click means the end of the task, however, the reward is always given in the position which was practised previously.

5. Now practise the same thing on your left side. In this case, as a signal walk very clearly on the left side of the path and take your left hand as the target.

Tip from a professional:

While initially the distractions are small and the distance large, over time you can demand more of your dog. With practice, he will then even be able to be reliably led past other dogs while not on the lead.

▼ Careful a rider — we will all walk on the right!

A Nice Back *Stay behind*

What resources? *Initially a human training assistant*

Requirements? *None*

The Task:

In general, I like to see my dog running in front of me. This means I can read his body language and take action in plenty of time if for example he starts to sniff around like mad. However, when I approach areas without a clear view – such as bends or where paths cross – it's better to have him behind me so that I have a good overview.

Always do things calmly!

Do things in small stages. You don't want to reprimand your dog, but rather praise him for the correct behaviour.
If the dogs are pushing forward next to you, it helps if you slow down.

Step by Step:

It's easiest to practise as a pair. As you don't have eyes in the back of your head, a training assistant is really useful. The body signal for "Stay behind!" is when my arms are stretched out to the side. They almost form a fence.

1. While you are blocking the path visually with your arms, your assistant will click or mark behind you when your dog is correctly staying only two or three steps behind you.

2. You have the treats and should throw them behind you on the click. This means that the expected behaviour of the dog is directed behind you.

3. In the next step, you go ahead like before. However, now the treats will land behind you only when you have scouted out the area without a clear view. This releases the dog again.

4. Use your training assistant for as long as possible. If you are on your own, a glance over your shoulder will have to be sufficient. My experience shows that walking more slowly holds dogs back more than attempting to stay in front by walking more quickly ahead of the dog.

▼ We are approaching the crossroads – that means: stay back!

Achoo! *Great service!*

What resources? *White fabric handkerchief or tissues, but they tear easily*

Requirements? *Retrieving, see page 150*

The Task:

When you "sneeze" (signal word "Achoo!"), your dog should pull a handkerchief out of your trouser pocket and put it in your hand. This is a nice retrieving task which will appeal to your audience.

What is shaping?

Shaping means that behaviour displayed by a dog through a click or marker word is captured and rewarded. Depending on the dog, this lucrative action is consciously demonstrated at an early or late stage.
Always progress with small steps and reward even minor attempts. Your dog needs experiences – give them to him!

Step by Step:

1. You throw the handkerchief on the floor and ask your dog to put it in your hand.
2. You put the handkerchief on a slightly higher surface (tree stump, bench) and let your dog retrieve it and put it in your hand.
3. You name the handkerchief "Achoo!"
4. The handkerchief is almost hanging completely out of your left trouser pocket and you ask your dog to take it out and put in your right hand by saying "Achoo!"
5. The tip of the handkerchief hanging out of your pocket becomes increasingly smaller and the dog has to make more of an effort to pull it out.
6. You use the other front trouser pocket so that he has to search for the handkerchief.
7. Then also use the back pockets for the handkerchief.

Tip from a professional:

If you are able to shape a sneeze with your dog you can create a nice behaviour chain. For example, you substantiate Luna's sneeze with the signal word "ill" so that you can ask: "Are you ill, Luna?", Luna sneezes, you say sympathetically that you are ill as well. You sneeze and Luna gives you your handkerchief. Everyone will be impressed with this clever and helpful dog and Luna will be really proud of all the attention!

▶ **When Nala** looks for the handkerchief, she has laughter on her side!

Good Idea *Who is the most creative?*

What resources? None
Requirements? None

The Task:

It's fun to encourage our dogs to be creative. Here they are allowed to suggest something to us for a change.

This way of operating is completely new to many dogs and expectations should be very low. Don't expect him to offer completely new forms of behaviour. But with a bit of luck at some point he will offer something, which will give you some new ideas. Perhaps this will really lead to a new trick – following an idea from your dog!

Step by Step:

1. As an exception, start immediately with the new signal word: "Do something!" to encourage him or simply "Good idea!"

2. Then almost everything which the dog offers will be clicked. Does he move a step backwards? Click! Does he look to the side? Click! Does he show you his familiar party pieces? Click! Does he lick his nose? Click! Your observation skills are required here.

3. Allow your dog to repeat things a few times (particularly as he has learned to repeat successful behaviour). But then let him know that you are asking for something new by saying "Carry on!"

4. As usual, you should not spend too long on this task. Finish with a particularly nice suggestion, give him lots of praise again for his good ideas and carry on. However, don't give up too quickly. Try again in short exercise sections and wait to see what happens.

Tip from a professional:

With a particularly talented dog who has learned to offer things independently, you can set the bar higher: every form of behaviour is allowed to be displayed only once. Or as a further enhancement, only reward behaviour which is really new.

◀ Is it my turn?

▶ Not bad, is it?

Sniffing Around *Always follow your nose*

What resources? A longer lead, if possible, a harness

Requirements? None

The Task:

There are days when you just want some peace and quiet for your dog and for you. Practise relaxing and let your dog sniff around to his heart's content while on the lead and on your walk.

Step by Step:

You have lots of opportunities for an interesting walk with a "freestyle snout":

- Deliberately go where lots of dogs have been previously. Male dogs in particular enjoy being able to follow their noses in peace for once.

- Your dog will also be grateful if you vary your walk. He loves variety for his nose — in the same way that we also don't want to read the same book over and over again.

- From time to time deliberately select places with exciting odours. Perhaps he might be allowed to sniff around a car park without any disruption for once — the next walk then doesn't have to be so far.

- Another exciting option is to let your dog lead you while he is on the lead! At crossroads encourage him with "Lead me!" Observe him very carefully and follow the smallest signals he makes in a certain direction.

- Our dogs' world of smells will always remain closed to us. Nevertheless, it can be interesting to allow ourselves to be led by our dogs. Perhaps this will give us an insight into their interests.

Tip from a professional:

For some dogs, pedestrians are simply too slow. If he knows the instruction "Lead me!", then he can also be accompanied by his owner on a bicycle without being on a lead. In general, dogs enjoy covering longer distances. Of course, while on the lead he must have learned that freedom on paths remains restricted; and we in turn must give him time to sniff in places he finds interesting.

▲ Simply unwind.

▼ Ahhh, Prada is allowed to sniff to her heart's content today!

Playing Sherpa The dog must contribute

What resources? *Items to carry*

Requirements? *None*

The Task:

Dogs with some retriever heritage can carry sticks or toys around with them with great perseverance and enthusiasm. If such a "carrying dog" belongs to you, you can also keep him busy in a way appropriate to his species.

Carrying things can also help animals who get excitable from environmental stimuli to become more relaxed. Chewing is a way of dealing with stress for some dogs. Therefore, satisfy his sweet tooth and give your nervous dog a task which relaxes him and helps to calm him down.

Employment for your dog's snout can also be good entertainment for other walkers. For example, I knew a retriever who always carried an old walking boot around with him. The people walking past definitely smiled at him! A dog who carries his own lead also stands out. Perhaps you can even make their enjoyment of carrying useful: for example, my large mongrel used to help me carry my groceries home. He could easily manage a kilo or a litre.

Step by Step:

1. Praise your dog when he carries his favourite toy with him of his own accord and introduce a term for this.

2. Now you can allow your creativity to run riot. Think about objects, which will make your dog into a popular figure. For example, he could carry his lead or a special basket. It's helpful to fold the lead over and fasten it with a band. With the basket, I pad out the handle a bit so it's more sturdy and more comfortable to carry.

3. Think about incorporating breaks because even the keenest animal needs some time out. A carrying dog is working and can't follow his dog-based interests. Work is fun, but everyone also needs a bit of downtime and free time!

A basket is not prey!

Carrying can reduce stress and help your dog to cope with difficult situations in a more relaxed way. However, some dogs start to regard the item they are carrying as prey, which has to be monitored. Therefore, observe your dog carefully and only let him play sherpa where it's appropriate.

▶ When Coco carries her lead, everyone smiles.

Games Involving Exercise

Ready for the Olympics!

Younger dogs in particular really enjoy exercise. If they can exercise in a controlled environment, we will bring motivation and enjoyment to their everyday lives and at the same time reduce their potential interest in chasing other wild animals. Go into the fresh air with open eyes and you will find lots of challenges suitable for dogs, which you can continually use as ideas for new games!

Twist and Turn   Turn around

What resources? None
Requirements? None

The Task:

Your dog should turn to the right or left next to you. This is a great exercise to introduce the hand target. Here the dog should learn to follow the human hand like a magnet, without it containing a treat. Even very young dogs can learn this.

Step by Step:

1. Lead your dog with a treat so that he turns round in a clockwise direction.
2. The treat is replaced with a movement of your hand. To do this, put your hand in the treat bag and guide your dog with your other empty hand. As soon as he has turned, say your reward word and feed him.
3. Instead of guiding him with your hand, it will be sufficient later to turn your finger slightly as a signal. A reward follows as usual!
4. Turning anticlockwise is taught in the same way. You can practise turning right and left at the same time or concentrate on one direction and then add the other later.

Tip from a professional:

You can use two different sounding signal words for the two turning directions, for example "turn" and "twist" and practise the trick without a hand signal. Perhaps your dog might also learn from a distance?

◀ **Whoops,** that was a bit too high.

▼ The young short-haired collie Billy likes to follow Joseph's hand because he has hidden a piece of cheese in it.

Obstacle Course — Tests of courage for genuine heroes

What resources? None
Requirements? None

The Task:

The whole world can become a playground for our dogs! While you are out, let your dog jump, climb, balance, crawl and lots of other things! In woods for example there are numerous tree stumps for jumping and balancing exercises. The second stage is on top of rocks and over ditches! Challenging surfaces such as grates, smooth flooring or difficult steps can be found in urban areas. There are posts, which can be navigated, small walls on which to balance or artworks which inspire movement games. Go through the world with open eyes and discover the opportunities!

Step by Step:

1. Look for a suitable "plaything" and think about some form of movement associated with it.
2. Initially guide your dog with treats in your hand and call the action: "Jump!"
3. Later a verbal instruction will be sufficient with a finger movement so that your dog can also climb on, go round or jump over things which are further away.
4. Praise your dog for his courage – he's bound to be thrilled with your amazement!

Tip from a professional:

The level of difficulty can be increased here without any limits. Let your imagination run riot! For example, how about allowing your dog to go up a smooth step backwards?

Only go on go!

An important point must be mentioned. Although your dog is allowed to point out opportunities to you (experienced dogs love developing their own ideas!), he is only allowed to put them into practice in response to your request. Initiative is never rewarded here! There is too great a risk that he will gleefully jump over a wall, behind which there is a steep drop. I am thinking for example of castle walls or walls on bridges!

Triathlon   *Leaping, crawling and going round*

What resources? None

Requirements? Area with park benches

The Task:

Benches are an extremely versatile form of "apparatus for dog sport". You can do so much with them. The first thing a dog usually learns is a "Jump!" The second option is to crawl underneath if it's high enough. Thirdly the triathlete can walk "round the outside".

Step by Step:

Dogs learn using a location-based approach. It will therefore be easier for your dog to associate the individual actions with different benches. Jumping will take place at one bench, the other one will be walked around and he can crawl under the third one.

1. At the beginning, entice him with treats until your dog has understood which movement is expected. Link the bench and a verbal signal with a certain movement of your hand: "Jump!" can be a movement upwards, "Through" a movement downwards and "Round the outside" moving your left arm clockwise.

2. If your dog can do all three tricks individually, you can ask a question by one bench. Get him to concentrate on himself and give very clear hand signals.

3. Keep a lookout for other suitable objects. For example, we have a large tyre set upright in concrete. Dogs can also jump through things like this, jump up and go round the outside. Perhaps there is a concrete pipe which also makes this possible?

Tips from a professional:

Try to send your dog from a distance. Another option is to work just verbally without any hand signals.

▲ "Jump!", and what comes next?

Just have fun!

If it doesn't work immediately, then simply try it again. The great thing about these activities is that there is no exam looming and this means the fun element won't disappear!

▼ Round the outside with a bit of oomph!

Round, Round, Get Around *Round the outside!*

What resources? *None*

Requirements? *Area with sheds, a tree, small garden*

The Task:

The dog learns to go round smaller or larger objects in response to a signal.

▶ **This game** is even more enjoyable if there are several dogs!

Step by Step:

1. Stand very close to a tree with your dog.
2. Now guide your dog with a hand target (see page 106) or treat behind the tree and entice him back to the front with your right hand. Success? Reward with a marker signal (see page 90) and treats!
3. Continue practising with both hands until he does it without any treats in your hand and in the end only moving your hand backwards is sufficient as a signal.
4. Try it a bit further away from the tree. The signal can be to point to the tree with the instruction "Round the outside!"
5. First of all, the distance becomes greater, then the object to go round. For example, look for a very small shed or a small rock.
6. Try to send your dog round barns or small fenced gardens!

A good reward for doing this quickly can be a toy thrown in the direction to follow.

Tips from a professional:

- Build the exercise up differently in an anticlockwise direction. Now you could say "Go around!", supported with a clear send movement with your right arm. Make your dog concentrate on himself and then send him round to the left and right on an alternating basis!

- Do you need an even greater challenge? Then send one dog round to the right and another dog round to the left.

113

▲ Around the back ...

▲ ... and back again!

Well Herded! *Herding game for herders*

What resources? *Several people later on*
Requirements? *None*

The Task:

While you are out for a walk, your dog runs round you when told to do so. It gets exciting if two people are walking or the whole family is out for a walk.

Herd if you can!

It's not easy to display the abilities of sheepdogs/herding dogs. Chasing games are much mpre playful rather than those involving herding. The point is for our sheepdogs not to "herd" passing cyclists or deer. But might they enjoy herding family members? Be careful as some sheepdogs can then tend to take herding people seriously. Observe your dog carefully and decide whether such games are the right thing for him!

Step by Step:

1. Guide your protector with a hand target (see page 106) or initially with a treat: your right hand guides him to the back and your left hand to the front again. As soon as he has popped back up in the front, use your marker signal (see page 90) to tell him: "That's right" and reward him.

2. Continue practising with both hands until it's also successful without any treats in your hand and lastly just the hand signal pointing to the back is sufficient.

3. Now walk closely next to your two-legged companion. The person walking on the right starts to guide the dog behind them with their right hand.

4. Their neighbour walking on the left continues the movement with their left hand and guides the dog back to the front again … Marker signal and a big reward!

5. Now the distance between the two dog lovers becomes larger. Is it still working?

Tip from a professional:

First let your dog walk round several people and then finally a small dispersed group of (dedicated) walkers.

▼ And now Jonny pops up in front again!

Slalom *Slalom through your legs*

What resources? *None*
Requirements? *None*

The Task:

Does your dog love games involving movement and would probably find an agility course exciting? Then why don't you treat him to this on your walk? You always have your legs with you to use as "slalom poles" ... and you can already start: your dog runs in a figure of eight around your legs – a task which is easy to learn and is particularly beneficial for older dogs because of the flowing movement of the back in both directions.

Step by Step:

1. Stand with your legs wide apart in front of your dog and guide him with a treat in your hand around your right leg and back between your legs from the back to the front. At the beginning you can emphasise every attempt with a marker signal and give a treat.

2. The movement is expanded by going round the left leg. The aim is to form a complete figure of eight.

3. Omit the treat over time so that your dog merely follows your guiding hand.

4. Instead of guiding with your hand, later moving your knee outwards with a slight movement of your hip will be sufficient. It becomes the signal to run under this knee and come back to the front. You can therefore sway elegantly from side to side, while your dog moves in a figure of eight around your legs.

Tip from a professional:

Now practise the slalom around your legs in a flowing forwards movement. This also works surprisingly well with really large dogs. Initially guide him with your hand again. Later one leg in front of the other will be sufficient as the signal. If you want to speed things up, then throwing a ball can be a good reward!

▼ Too big for slaloming? Never!

Impulse Control
be Careful!

Impulse control games are very exciting for your four-legged friend and at the same time a wonderful exercise for the serious matter of encountering something while off the lead. Dogs are hunters of prey and really love it when games closely reflect this situation.

At such times, it's then a huge challenge for the animals to work with their human owners and always exciting. The reward is then pure, unadulterated action!

Catch it! *Caught in mid-flight*

What resources? *Food or a light toy*
Requirements? *None*

The Task:

Flying food is particularly attractive for your dog, as it satisfies his desire to hunt. The food reward has a higher value because of this. Also, if a dog has a tendency to sometimes snatch the treat from your hand a bit roughly, the owner is pleased if the food can be thrown to the dog!

Careful!

Please don't throw balls or other objects which are too small into your dog's mouth. He might swallow them.

Step by Step:

1. Not all dogs are born to catch! They often watch the treat flying in the air until it lands on the ground and then pick it up. Your first task is now to throw accurately. This will be warmly welcomed by a slightly open mouth!

2. Sometimes your dog will suddenly understand what the game is about if the object moves a bit more slowly. Try it with a light soft toy, flannel or knotted cloth. Once it has been caught, the penny often drops!

3. It frequently works surprisingly well if you sit several dogs who know each other together and throw them bits of food in turn calling out their names. Start with a bit of distance between the dogs to see whether there is any resource aggression, in other words food envy. Once the dogs know this game, they can also sit closely next to each other. This is always a good way of spending time if you are waiting for something.

Tips from a professional:

- Try to place a treat on your dog's nose and after a short wait throw it up in the air and give your dog the familiar signal word "Catch it!" so he can catch it. This has been shown to work well with food that is not too light so that it remains stable on the nose and is also easy for the dog to catch.

- Depending on the size of his mouth and toy, a dog can also catch several items at once. If he understands "Hold", you can try to throw a second object. Sometimes it also helps if your dog understands what is desired!

▼ Look sharp! I've got it!

Balla-balla! Colourful ball games

What resources? A ball (preferably on a string)

Requirements? The dog loves balls and already knows a simple "Stay!"

The Task:

Lots of dogs love balls. Use this enjoyment to make exercise fun, while also promoting thinking and strengthening impulse control. In this task your dog will learn to react to a ball only in response to a request to do so.

Step by Step:

1. Sit your dog down and go back a bit. Move the ball slightly in your hands. If your dog stays seated, call out "Okay!" loudly and cheerfully, turn around and throw the ball.

2. Increase the excitement by moving further away from your dog and making the ball more attractive by swinging it around in front of your dog's nose.

3. If your dog gets up too early, don't tell him off and correct him – the ball simply vanishes silently under your armpit. On the next attempt you should reconsider the level of difficulty and possibly reduce it. In this way you will work out a way of challenging your dog at a level he can cope with. Excessive expectations are frustrating for both of you. Success makes things fun – even at a simple level.

Tips from a professional:

Is simply throwing the ball and letting it be brought back challenging enough? Always think about different tasks to allow playing with a ball to become a reward. Here are a few ideas:

- Throw two (or even more) balls in various directions while your dog is sitting down and watching. Send him to the ball which was thrown first and only then to the other one.

- You now dance wildly in front of the dog who is sitting or lying down, waving the ball enticingly in the air and making all the movements as if you are going to throw a ball, without actually throwing it. Then finally comes the liberating signal "Okaaaaaay".

- If your dog loves balls, practise a "Sit" from a distance and throw the ball as a reward. My dogs really enjoy it if I pretend to throw a ball, they dash off and then have to sit down in the distance first and then I throw the ball as a reward in the opposite direction.

Take a break sometimes!

Some dogs are addicted to the stimulus of movement. We want to make the most of this but not overdo it. Therefore, make sure you offer running games only in certain doses. Even more than with other games, it's important to stop here when things are going well. Practise a hand signal for "Break" and keep to it consistently once you have given it.

▼ Traditional: a child, a dog and a ball.

One, Two, Three, Hide! *Playing hiding games*

What resources? *Possibly a whistle*
Requirements? *Area with no overview*

The Task:

We play this simple but always exciting game almost every day: you make your dogs sit down, walk away behind a tree and whistle (or call) the dogs to come over. The dogs not only love it but also learn a lot. Firstly, they should practise sitting down quietly while the person moves away. Secondly, and this is the major learning effect – they are finally allowed to run over to their owner when the whistle sounds.

It's important to "upload" the whistle (or call) repeatedly in a positive way, in other words to use it in situations when the dog really wants to come. On the other hand, if we only whistle him back when he has something exciting in his head, he quickly learns to regard the whistle as a brake on his fun. How great that this game continually gives us the opportunity to condition the return as a positive experience.

Step by Step:

1. In its simplest form, this game can already be played with puppies. Let your dog sit, slowly turn around and whistle for him to come towards you. Go one step back and repeat the call. Increase the level of difficulty so slowly that your dog doesn't make any mistakes. If he stands up too early, go back one learning step.

2. If he already sits down briefly, then go back slowly and disappear behind a nearby tree. Now whistle for him to come towards you. Of course, there must always be a good reward!

3. Soon you can look for a real place to hide. Sit your dog down somewhere so he won't be able to see you, for example near a bend in the path or behind a wooden pole. Depending on the location and dog, you can now move away and hide. Duck behind a bush, stand behind a tree and wait a few seconds before your whistle.

Coming back is worthwhile!

Calls to come back are always highly rewarded. Therefore, keep a special treat as often as possible for this game. Of course, a dog who likes a rough game of tug could also be rewarded with that.

▲ A whistle ...

▲ ... and the fun begins!

Come Here! But please one after the other

What resources? *At the start, it's best to have one person per dog*

Requirements? *None*

The Task:

Calling games are enjoyable and reaffirm calling back. At the same time, you are demanding lots of impulse control and concentration.

Step by Step:

1. Sit two or more dogs next to each other. It's much easier for them if a few people are also involved. Each person stands opposite a dog, looks for eye contact and makes a hand movement to indicate "Stay!"

2. Very gently the youngest or least trained dog is called (to their owner). Then the second and so on.

3. A nice extension for advanced dogs is to sit the dogs down in order. With a bit of practice, it will be possible for the dog at the back to be called first. He will therefore run past his friends who are sitting further forward and who must ignore him. Remember that every call should be highly rewarded!

Tip from a professional:

It's even more difficult if only one person is leading several dogs. Sit them down next to each other and try to call them individually.

It's surprisingly difficult for these clever animals to distinguish their names by sound. It would be helpful to introduce a different hand signal for each dog. Dogs find it much easier to read body language than distinguish between verbal signals. As we humans communicate differently, it's important to always remember this.

The hand helps

Among other things, also with deaf dogs, it's helpful to introduce a hand signal for the call to come back. This can for example be a raised hand, which is lowered to the thigh when you call out.

▼ Ready, steady, go!

Chase the Prey ... but not immediately

What resources? *Toy with a string attached, stick*

Requirements? *The dog should know "Sit" and "Out"*

The Task:

A home-made play rod is a really attractive toy for dogs who are interested in catching prey. At the same time, it can be used for impulse control exercises.

Step by Step:

1. Tie the toy to a suitable stick you have found on your walk. Let your dog sit down and move the toy carefully and slowly to and fro in front of him.

2. Then follow this by calling out "Okay!" and he is then allowed to catch his "prey". Depending on the level of training, please proceed in very small steps. If your dog's impulse control is not yet that extensive, move the toy slowly and give him the pleasure of the chase after only a short wait. As soon as he gets up too early without permission, you have progressed too quickly. In this case, discontinue and start again, but this time with few expectations regarding his self-control.

3. As soon as your dog is allowed to chase after the toy, create a short hunting sequence. He is allowed to scamper about, jump and finally reach the toy.

4. Now call him to you and give him the prey or exchange it for something of higher or equal value – depending on your dog's level of training. The task should be highly rewarded with food or a tugging game.

5. Please remember that a play rod chase will really push up your dog's level of excitement and completely tire him out at the same time. Only use this activity sparingly and in short sequences. In this way your dog will love this exciting game even more!

▲ For once I'm allowed to be a **wild animal!**

Tip from a professional:

Try to bring your dog out of the "Chase" into a "Sit". He is allowed to jump up and continue chasing in response to your "Okay!"

▼ It can't be any more exciting.

Works of Art
Lots of Tricks for Talented Dogs

Tricks are fun – and are extremely useful. Dogs who have mastered tricks are objects of affection and we definitely need those nowadays! Even a cautious child is more likely to approach dogs if they have mastered amusing tricks. Although for external effect, tricks are also just as useful as any training for the dog-person relationship because both will discover that learning is fun!

Target! *Target games*

What resources? *None*

Requirements? *None*

The Task:

Our dogs can learn how to touch targets (objects) with their noses or paws. Looked at this way, our hand becomes a paw target, when our dog learns how to give us a paw.

For example, when you are on a walk, dogs can indicate trees by climbing up them with their front paws. However, for older dogs a nose nudge is also an option as a pointer.

Some suitable targets outside are for example tree stumps, marker stones, junction boxes, posts, distinctive stones …

Step by Step:

1. First the dog learns to climb onto an object with his front paws. To do this, take a treat, entice him up and reward him immediately when he has done this.

2. Now try to get him to climb up using your empty hand.

3. Stand two paces away from the object and send him to climb up it. If he understands this, for example call the action "Show!"

4. The distance becomes greater and you practise sending him in the right direction with a pointing movement.

5. When your dog doesn't immediately find the target you intended, regard this as part of the exercise to direct him correctly from a distance. Enjoy his success when he has managed it!

Tip from a professional:

Practise letting your dog stand by the object until you give your okay. It's helpful to introduce a sound which tells your dog: "What you have just done is fantastic, please continue doing the things I tell you!" This sound is called the keep-going signal and can be a "lalalalala". I call out "gogogogo". Anything is an option.

"Wrong" and "Shame"

And when things don't work out? I have two words for negative feedback: "Wrong" and "Shame". Wrong means he is not offering the right thing. Help him to have successful experiences quickly! If he can actually do it, I finish with "Shame". No reward, no more enjoyable tasks, but also no unpleasant consequences. On the next attempt, you should lower the level of difficulty slightly.

▼ Paws up high!

The Trick Bench *For a relaxing break*

What resources? None

Requirements? Bench or tree stump lying on the ground

The Task:

Dogs learn in a very location-based way. Dogs who enjoy learning like to link certain places with learning experiences. This is the reason why lots of dogs are enthusiastic about going to the dog training ground. They know precisely that something interesting will happen again there.

Perhaps there is somewhere on your usual dog walk which is suitable for a short break. For example, this could be a bench. If you decide to work on a nice trick at this spot on a regular basis, your dog will be thrilled and you can enjoy a short break.

As an example of work for your dog while you are sitting comfortably, I suggest the hand target here. Something like this can also easily be practised when spending a long time in a restaurant.

Step by Step:

1. Hold your right hand upright in front of your dog. As soon as your dog shows some interest and moves closer, mark this behaviour with a click or your reward word.

2. The dog will have made the link and will nudge your hand wherever you are holding it out towards him. This trick helps for example in situations in which he is stressed and can be distracted with a simple task – this often has a better effect than a treat. For example, the signal word can be "Touch".

Tip from a professional:

As the next step, practise the "chin touch". You hold the palm of your hand out towards your dog and get him to place his head on your hand in small steps. A "cheek touch" can be created when your hand is upright.

◀ The chin touch – very gentle.

▼ Daisy is being a "bunny rabbit"!

The Naysayer *It's raining, so what?!*

What resources? None

Requirements? None

The Task:

Even well-behaved dogs find things difficult these days. The media whip up fears and children often don't have an opportunity to learn how to get to know dogs correctly.

I use every opportunity to overcome prejudices so that children can have positive experiences with dogs. Without realising it, little ones can learn how to handle dogs at the same time and the animals can experience children in a positive way.

Little tricks which children enjoy (and astonish adults!) have proved to be very helpful. Our favourite is the dog who shakes his head to say "No!".

Yes or no?

It's much easier to learn a "Yes!" and that's why I practise it much later when the "No!" is already firmly established. A "Yes!" is a bark. I practise it with questions starting with "Do you think …" Therefore, you can then ask: "Do you think Julia is nice?" and the dog will bark a cheerful "Yes!", "Do you like cucumbers?" – head-shaking "No!"

Step by Step:

1. On a rainy day set off armed with your dog, food and possibly a clicker. As soon as your dog shakes himself, click or mark as immediately as possible and reward him. You are then trying to make your dog aware of a certain type of behaviour by reaffirming it (shaping, see page 96). He will understand this very quickly with the trigger of rain and frequently shake himself. You will see how exciting walks in the rain suddenly become!

2. The difficulty for your dog is now also to be able to shake himself without the trigger of rain. My dogs finally understood it on a day with wet meadows. Only half of the dog was wet – yet it was enough to have a shake. Perhaps wet paws on a short lawn will be sufficient?

3. Once he has understood what you want, introduce a signal word. What works for me is for him to answer any questions starting with "Do you like …" by using "No". For example, in response to "Do you like rain?", he should shake his head. You can now find other words such as tomatoes, crocodiles, etc. Vary the words and look forward to spending time with your talking dog!

Tip from a professional:

Highly talented dogs can learn to link "Yes" and "No" with almost invisible body signals. For example, think about a gesture with your thumb and your foot to get the right answer. Your dog will gain lots of admirers!

▼ Nala always shakes herself a lot after rolling around. Now there's a reward every time she does it.

Catch the Dog *Come into my arms!*

What resources? *None*

Requirements? *A person who can cope with the weight of the dog*

The Task:

If your dog likes jumping into your lap, you can teach him to jump into your arms when instructed to do so as an impressive feat. The important thing is for the dog not only to jump up but also towards you with the expectation of being caught. Only in this way will you be able to catch him securely.

Step by Step:

1. Find various seating options in the wood and encourage your dog to jump into your lap. As a visual signal, use your extended arms ready to catch him from the outset.

2. A wood is a perfect location to find a slightly raised seat. Sit up as straight as possible and let your dog jump.

3. The possible seats should get higher so that you are no longer sitting completely horizontally, but standing slightly at a slant (half-sitting). Your arms will increasingly support your dog.

4. From an almost horizontal position, you work yourself into an almost vertical position. Your dog will get used to being caught by you.

5. For the first few vertical jumps, you can always still lean on a tree.

6. You stand in an open space like a meadow and confidently catch the dog jumping towards you. Congratulations on this spectacular trick!

Tip from a professional:

If your dog is clever enough, he can jump down into your arms from a wooden post. Select the height so that your dog can be caught safely!

◀ **Directly on you** – first on your lap.

▼ Caught you!

Cool Paw *Give the rear paws*

What resources? None
Requirements? Park benches

The Task:

Perhaps you have already noticed how horses' hooves are scraped out. They stand there patiently and it's sufficient to tap them so that they lift up their hind hooves. Of course, our dogs can also learn to do this! Another great task for our "trick bench".

Step by Step:

1. Start with your dog's right hind leg. Tap it lightly and mark even the smallest movement. At the beginning, this will usually be a step backwards.

2. Patiently practise some more and try to shape the behaviour in the desired direction. Think about the horses – they have also learned this and are certainly not superior learners to our dogs!

3. Only practise in very short sequences. If he has moved his rear paw three times, this is sufficient. Always try to finish on an attempt which is as good as possible!

4. Only add the selected signal word when your dog demonstrates the behaviour.

Tip from a professional:

If you have an extremely talented dog, you can give all four legs a name, I suggest "one, two, three, four". Now you can let him give you his paws in turn!

Just be patient!

Some tricks simply need time. Give yourself and your dog this time! There is really no pressure to be successful. I have already been working with my animals on some tricks for years – sometimes with longer breaks, sometimes every day. This makes me even prouder when the dog quite surprisingly suddenly understands what it's all about!

▲ The first step has been achieved: "one" ... and so on.

▼ Daisy is proud of her skills!

My Dog, the Model *Photo greetings*

What resources? *Initially twigs, later flowers or other photogenic items & a friend with a camera*

Requirements? *None*

The Task:

Our dogs are grateful to be photo models. With the corresponding practice, they are extremely patient and of course they are always attractive! This trick will help you take even better pictures. Even if you are not doing the photography yourself, you will always find someone you know, who will be happy to take pictures of your well-trained dog. Naturally you can also practise this without a camera on your daily walks.

Step by Step:

1. The basic exercise for a four-legged photo model is "Stay!" Your dog should stay sitting or lying down. Therefore, tell him to sit and move one or two steps backwards, bend down a bit (good photos of dogs are always from a lower position), stand up again and reward your dog. It's up to you whether he should stay until you come back over to him or whether he is allowed to come to you after the reward signal.

2. Now increase the distance and move even lower towards the floor. But hold your hand in front of your face like a camera. We call this exercise "Photo".

3. Practise standing, sitting and lying down. The aim is to achieve a "frozen" photo model, who stands or sits calmly and only moves his head.

4. Practise sitting or standing with several dogs, who are touching each other. Usually, they like to have their own individual space, but this isn't good for photos. We often practise this contact sitting with "Together!"

Tips from a professional:

Ideas for advanced photo models:

- A flower in your dog's mouth is a beautiful image for photographic greetings. Initially practise with a small twig, later with a green flower stem, then with a flower. Carry on as above: go back a few paces and bend down before you give the trigger signal and the flower is allowed to fall onto the floor or into your hand.

- Other greetings ideas include a decorated basket, a gift bag with a pretty print, or a flag.

- You can take beautiful portraits of a dog who has already mastered "Down" and lays his head down on the floor. Practise with a target, for example a sponge which has been cut up. Place the target in your open hand and practise the chin touch (see page 134), then onto the floor. Cut the sponge into increasingly smaller pieces until a signal word is sufficient.

▼ Who wouldn't enjoy receiving a greetings card like this?

Into the Blue   True blue

What resources?   None

Requirements?   An area with blue objects

The Task:

For a long time, it was assumed that dogs could only see shades of grey. It is now clear that they see colours, but their eyes tend to be more geared towards light sensitivity and motion vision rather than colours. While dogs lack red receptors, they see the colour blue particularly well.

Keep your eyes open on your dog walks. Are there any blue objects? Sometimes food bins or plastic wrappers are bright blue. Try to point them out to your dogs.

Step by Step:

1. If your dog has already learned to point out objects, he will quickly understand that you always want the same (blue!) things to be identified on your daily walks. As pointing behaviour, you can encourage everything which your dog offers to you: for example nose contact, paw contact or barking. However, once the pointing behaviour has been introduced, it should be retained.

2. Introduce the signal word "Blue!" and practise it regularly with as many different objects as possible.

3. It gets really exciting when you are in an unfamiliar area and find new blue objects. Has your dog understood this? Send your dog off and find out whether he knows what you mean. Really celebrate if he points out something correctly.

Turning things blue!

Of course, you can also integrate blue practice objects into your garden or other private spaces. Spray or paint stones or bits of wood blue and distribute them around. However, you should then wait several weeks before you use them as blue markers. Otherwise, your dog will quickly learn to identify the odour of the paint! Other colours which dogs can also identify easily are yellow and white.

▼ Jonny has learned to identify the colour blue and point to it.

Nose Work

There's a Scent in the Air

Our four-legged friends experience their environment largely via their noses. It's fascinating to see how they give us an insight into what they can achieve through their noses via search games. At the same time, the curious animals show us how much they adore search games.

It soon becomes obvious that a relatively short period of nose work exerts our dogs just as much as a long walk: we should definitely include search games into our entertainment repertoire!

Finders, Keepers *Whoops, lost it!*

What resources? *Treat bag or other food dummy, handkerchief*

Requirements? *Retrieving (see page 150)*

The Task:

A wonderful opportunity for your dog to become excitable is occasionally "losing" items. You start with items filled with food such as the food dummies you can buy, school pencil cases, key cases with a zip or a purse.

Very keen for a finder's reward

This is actually a very practical trick because my dogs have already unintentionally brought me gloves which I had misplaced and even once my reading glasses! However, some dogs keep such a beady eye on their scatterbrained owners that it's difficult to unobtrusively lose a handkerchief!

Step by Step:

1. While you are out strolling with your dog, you "lose" his treat bag. Three metres further on, you are horrified to discover this and look for it together with your dog. If he knows about retrieving, he will quickly understand the new game! When he lifts up the small case/item, of course he is handsomely rewarded from inside the case.

2. Now the distance becomes greater until the bag is out of sight. As a signal, I use a horrified "Ah, lost!" with a tap on my heart as a hand signal, which has worked well.

3. You can quickly move on to other objects from the treat bag. A tissue has proved excellent because its white colour makes it stand out. You can easily lose lots of objects and the only condition is that it has your scent.

Tips from a professional:

- Vary the distances for the lost item. An object very close by then suddenly becomes extremely difficult, which the enthusiastic sniffing nose will quickly run past.

- Also try with items which are more difficult to carry: an old mobile phone, for example, or a bunch of keys, which is hard to lift. Most dogs also dislike putting metal in their mouths.

▼ Not so easy to lose a handkerchief without Joy noticing.

Let's Search *Search for the scrunchie*

What resources? *Initially a treat bag or a food dummy, later scrunchies*

Requirements? *None*

The Task:

Children aren't the only ones who are surprised by how our dogs can find objects on their own with their nose. This game is then double the fun: the hiding for us and the finding for the dog.

Pencil cases, key cases with a zip or an old purse can also be used as a food dummy for example.

Step by Step:

The condition for our search is retrieving. If he isn't familiar with this yet, he will first have to learn that the food bag can be opened only with the help of his owner (point 1 and 2).

1. Show your four-legged friend the mystery bag with its beautiful scent and place it directly in front of him. Hopefully he will lower his nose with interest – and you can immediately click this and reward it.

2. If he then takes it in his mouth, this action is reaffirmed. But he doesn't have to hand it over: the click with the offer of some sausage is sufficient so that he drops it. Practise this until he lifts the bag he has dropped and lets go of it near your hand or ideally hands it over to you.

3. For the next step (and for bright minds who can already retrieve), tie your dog up, show him the filled case and "hide" it in full sight and very close. Now go back to your dog and send him off with a "Search!" If he brings the dummy back to you, there will be a reward jackpot!

4. The hiding can quickly become more exciting. Children are really amazed when the clever animal can find a bag quickly again among the leaves!

5. If your dog has learned the rules of the game, he will soon be able to transfer them to other hidden objects. I like colourful scrunchies, which are easy to bring with me and are also easy to fix onto twigs and branches. Your dog will still more or less be able to see white, blue or yellow scrunchies. Red ones are only visible to us and your dog will only be able to follow his nose for those.

Tips from a professional:

The opportunities to make the search game more difficult are endless. Here are two ideas:

- Let your dog sit down ("Sit!" and "Stay!") and wait while your hide the object.

- Choose items which are hidden higher up. About up to knee height has worked well for me. The higher it is, the more difficult it is because the scent is then sometimes very difficult for the dog to locate.

▼ Found it!

Where is he? *Dog looks for person*

What resources? *A second person, a well-fitting harness and a lead about 8 metres long, a small plastic container with high-quality food. Two mobile phones are useful.*

Requirements? *None*

The Task:

The dog has to find family members and friends in a straightforward area.

Man-trailing

If you and your dog enjoy this type of nose work, you can progress further under the supervision of a man-trailing group. Here you can then also learn how to search for and find strangers following a scent target. It's challenging, but fascinating teamwork, in which the person guiding the dog is completely reliant on his four-legged friend.

Step by Step:

1. A family member or friend shows your dog on the lead a plastic container with enticing food. While you let the dog watch, the "victim" moves away with the container and hides behind a nearby tree.

2. Send your dog after him with a "Look for Billy" and usually he won't have to be asked twice! He will really enjoy seeing Billy again, reinforced by the treat!

3. You will now be able to play the game of hide and seek out of the direct line of sight. Let your dog watch how the "victim" moves away.

4. The distance can now become longer, but I very much recommend progressing slowly. Learn how to read your dog and become a team with him. Are there signs that he has lost the trail? Then stay close to "green" backgrounds and have lots of successful experiences before you think about increasing the level of difficulty.

Tip from a professional:

Of course, when looking for a person, the demands can be increased endlessly: you can search on tarmac, the distractions can become greater and the trail older.

▼ Lucky and Joseph love playing hide and seek!

Picnic on the Grass *Bon appetit!*

What resources? *Food*
Requirements? *None*

The Task:

Take your dog's food outside for a change, serve it to him while you are out and combine it with a search.

Step by Step:

1. If your dog is being fed with pet food, this doesn't have to happen in a bowl at home. Take a handful of food and throw it up in the air so it lands on the grass. Piles of leaves or a bush also work well. Of course, people who feed their dogs with fresh food will also find something suitable.

   Even a fast eater will suddenly search and eat calmly. If dogs don't display any particular resource aggression, several dogs can also have a "picnic" together – this is really nice in the garden at home, above all when there's no time for anything else or the poor animal has to be careful because he is injured.

   A very attractive option is also to coat the coarse bark of a tree with soft food. He will be excited!

2. Let your dog watch how the food is distributed and only begin eating after a start signal.

3. Call him back in between to reward him with an even better treat!

▲ **Everyone** likes this!

Bon appetit!

Former street dogs, whose previous lives often only consisted of the search for food and who sometimes find it difficult to motivate themselves for anything else, can be kept busy in a species-appropriate way.

▼ Looking for food.

Show me! *Searching for items by pointing*

What resources? *A bag with food or a toy with a string, an additional lead*

Requirements? *None*

The Task:

For this game the dog does not have to be able to retrieve. It is associated with the work of search and rescue dogs. In this case, the dog also doesn't retrieve the victim but shows where it is – usually through barking, but other ways are also possible.

▲ **Now** I'm not letting it out of my sight any more!

Step by Step:

1. Take one of your dog's favourite toys or make a new one interesting. Soft toys are very good for this. This toy is now tied to a branch just out of reach.

2. If the dog shows interest and tries to reach it, the first attempt is already marked and rewarded. A good tugging game with the toy is a great reward at this point. Some dogs prefer food from the food bag – we should be guided completely by the dog's preferences here!

3. Now the dog should learn to point. Lots of dogs find it easiest to bark. Often, they can be prompted to do this with an action and they are only too happy to join in. On the first bark, take the toy down enthusiastically and play with your dog or reward him with food.

4. If he has understood, tie the "rescuer" up and fasten the soft toy within the line of sight.

5. Now go back to the dog and send him off. If he jumps towards the object and starts to bark, this should be reaffirmed as quickly as possible. Some dogs will also come back to you and guide you. This can also be a form of pointing behaviour to be promoted.

6. Now the hiding can become more exciting. Have fun hiding and searching!

Tips from a professional:

Once again you can slightly increase the excitement: for example, try to let your dog sit down on his own ("Sit!" and "Stay!"), while you hide the toy. Or, if your dog barks to point, encourage persistent barking until you reach your dog.

◀ Jonny has found the toy!

Geocaching *Treasure hunt with your dog*

What resources? *GPS, initially possibly a plastic container*

Requirements? *None*

The Task:

Geocaching is becoming increasingly popular as a leisure activity for the whole family. With the help of information on the internet and a GPS, this is a search for hidden treasure like a paper chase. If geocaching is new to you, you can find out a lot about it on the internet. Even if you are already an experienced geocacher, why don't you let your dog search for a change? With a bit of training, you can train your dog to become a caching dog: finding man-made objects, which lots of geocachers already have in their hands, in a natural environment is a great challenge for our dogs!

Always take it slowly!

Don't expect to have a fully trained caching dog very quickly. Remember how long it takes with daily practice to train a drug sniffing dog! Simply have fun searching and finding together! Enjoy the process.

Step by Step:

1. Caches simply hidden under tree roots or behind stones are suitable for a cache hunt with your dog. The most important thing is something hidden at the height of your dog's nose. Initially you need caches, which an experienced geocacher can already identify as such from a distance, for example a plastic container. Now send your dog off and mark every time he gets close. Then find the cache to great applause and show it to your dog.

2. Take the plastic container in your hand and reaffirm every nose nudge with food. Your dog should learn that interest in the container will be rewarded with food.

3. If you do this continually at various different caches, your dog will generalise what it is all about. Finally, every location of a find and every container will smell differently to him, but the strange objects associated with people in nature remain the same.

4. Now it's about shaping pointing behaviour. Observe whether you see the start of a form of behaviour which you can reinforce. Opportunities are, for example, scratching on the hidden object or locating it. Initially react to the smallest sign and praise your dog excessively! If you discover your dog can't reach the cache, simply hide it again under a few leaves to ensure a successful experience.

Tip from a professional:

While you should initially ensure that the search area is very small, you can extend the distance for a dog who has understood the game.

◀ Nala also thinks treasure hunts are exciting.

Resources

Further Reading

- Albers, Marion: *Filmreife Hundetricks. Tricktraining – nicht nur für angehende Filmhunde.* Verlag Eugen Ulmer 2018.
- del Amo, Celina: *Die neue Spassschule für Hunde. Spielen, tricksen, clickern.* Verlag Eugen Ulmer 2009
- del Amo, Celina: *Spiel- und Spassschule für Hunde. Über 200 Tricks und Übungen.* Verlag Eugen Ulmer 2012
- del Amo, Celina: *Abenteuer für Hunde. Spiel und Spass unterwegs.* Verlag Eugen Ulmer 2011
- Hesel, Lynn: *Apportierspiele. Dummyarbeit Schritt für Schritt.* Verlag Eugen Ulmer 2009
- Jakob, Anja: *Treibball. Vom Spiel zum Turniersport.* Kynos Verlag 2013
- Lenz, Corinna: *Hundespielzeug einfach selber machen.* Verlag Eugen Ulmer 2013
- Rauch, Liane: *Mein Einstein auf vier Pfoten. Kreative Bindungs- und Intelligenzspiele für Hunde.* Verlag Eugen Ulmer 2016
- Sondermann, Christina: *Einfach schnüffeln! Nasenspiele für den Hundealltag.* Verlag Eugen Ulmer 2017
- Sondermann, Christina: *Denksport für Hunde. Knobelspiele schnell und einfach selbstgemacht.* Verlag Eugen Ulmer 2017
- Spyrka, Frederike: *Hundetricks mit Nala. Vom Straßenhund zum Fernsehstar.* Verlag Eugen Ulmer 2019
- Sundance, Kyra: *101 Hundetricks.* Verlag Eugen Ulmer 2009
- Sundance, Kyra: *51 Tricks für junge Hunde.* Verlag Eugen Ulmer 2012
- Sundance, Kyra: *10-Minuten-Spiele für Hunde.* Verlag Eugen Ulmer 2012

Websites

- www.anjajakob.com
  Homepage of the author Anja Jakob with information on her courses, workshops and seminars on keeping dogs busy/entertained
- www.kalalassies.de
  Homepage of the author Cordula Weiss with information on short-haired collies, dog breeding and lots of ideas to keep dogs busy/entertained
- www.meinherzbellt.de/die-video-interviews/
  Free interviews, also by the author Anja Jakob, on a large number of interesting dog topics
- www.hey-fiffi.com
  Videos and articles with new suggestions and ideas, also by the author Anja Jakob, all about dogs and training
- www.spass-mit-hund.de
  Homepage of Christina Sondermann with lots of ideas on keeping dogs busy/entertained
- www.dogityourself.com
  Community website of Corinna Lenz with instructions on how to make toys yourself and more for dogs